organizational storytelling
FOR LIBRARIANS

organizational storytelling
FOR LIBRARIANS

USING STORIES FOR EFFECTIVE LEADERSHIP

KATE MAREK

AMERICAN LIBRARY ASSOCIATION
CHICAGO 2011

Kate Marek is a professor at Dominican University's Graduate School of Library and Information Science, where she teaches in the areas of technology and policy. She has worked as a library consultant and in all types of library organizations, and she writes in the areas of libraries, technology, and teaching.

Printed in the United States of America
15 14 13 12 11   5 4 3 2 1

While extensive effort has gone into ensuring the reliability of the information in this book, the publisher makes no warranty, express or implied, with respect to the material contained herein.

Note that any URLs referenced in this volume, which were valid at the time of first print publication, may have changed prior to electronic publication.

ISBN: 978–0-8389–1079–5

Library of Congress Cataloging-in-Publication Data
Marek, Kate.
    Organizational storytelling for librarians : using stories for effective leadership / Kate Marek.
        p. cm.
    Includes bibliographical references and index.
    ISBN 978-0-8389-1079-5 (alk. paper)
    1. Communication in library administration. 2. Storytelling. 3. Communication in organizations. 4. Leadership. I. Title.
    Z678.M33 2011
    025.1—dc22
                                2010033485

Cover design by Karen Sheets de Gracia. Text design in Georgia and Andika Basic by Chelsea McGorisk and Karen Sheets de Gracia.

♾ This paper meets the requirements of ANSI/NISO Z39.48-1992 (Permanence of Paper).

ALA Editions also publishes its books in a variety of electronic formats. For more information, visit the ALA Store at www.alastore.ala.org and select eEditions.

For my father, who is a consummate storyteller,
a compassionate listener, and a true guiding light

contents

introduction

I HAVE BEEN a proponent of using literature to teach for many years. The value of the vicarious experience we get from fiction is endless; I learned, for example, about American frontier history from Laura Ingalls Wilder's Little House books and about the English countryside (and about healing) from Frances Hodgson Burnett's *The Secret Garden*. As an adult I continue to learn so much about people and cultures through literature. We can extend that learning through discussion, applying the characters' successes and failures to our own understanding of life.

A strong parallel to my work with the power of literature is the sister concept of the power of narrative. The fine points of the similarities and differences between literature, fiction, and narrative are not important here. What is important is that my awareness of narrative led to a discovery of a fairly new facet of this huge part of life that is story: the power of narrative within the daily workings of an organization, and particularly for enhancing leadership.

Today organizational storytelling is an area of keen interest in the business community. Stephen Denning and Annette Simmons are among the best-known authors in this area, both of whom came from strong business backgrounds and who themselves began only hesitantly to embrace the power of story for corporate America. Denning has been especially successful in building a corporate following, although his background with the World

Bank did not exactly grease the skids for his initial forays into the use of story at work. He consistently retells his experience of the first time he ditched his PowerPoint graphs for a personal narrative to describe a significant World Bank service gap. He was understandably quite panicked about trying something so dramatically different in front of a very large and traditional World Bank executive audience, and yet he knew he needed to find a new way to communicate. His brief story about the impact of a knowledge network for medical information, told through the experiences of individuals rather than through numbers, was wildly successful at changing the direction of World Bank policies and helped forever change the development of knowledge management at the bank.[1]

As I continued to read more of the literature on organizational storytelling, I knew it made sense, and I knew others could do it effectively. I wasn't convinced, however, that I could do it. I decided to try. Rather than pouring out my life story, which I think is a fear we all have when we think about opening up or talking about ourselves, I decided to tell pieces of my "library story." I brought to my mind memories of library experiences throughout my life, both good and bad. I worked on converting those memories into language and images, so I could both talk about the memory and paint a verbal picture for my listeners.

I chose a few stories and a few captive audiences of graduate library school students, and I began to experiment. Almost immediately, the difference was amazing. For example, rather than tell a group of incoming students where I got my degree and what library jobs I had had, I told them of an early experience as a young girl, visiting a public library in the summer with my mother. I described the harsh Texas heat and the cool, air-conditioned public library, and the sense of wonder and security I had in the midst of the books and the building. Each time I told the story, I thought of more connections from my experience to what I wanted to convey to my students: that I had been a beneficiary of a strong library system in a country of strong libraries, but that as I grew older I realized this was not the case for all citizens, for all communities, or for all nations. I could use the same story to talk about "library as place," the changing nature of library services, and other timely issues. And as I understood my own story more, my listeners also understood more about libraries.

The power of story is within us all, and it is not just about telling tall tales or classical myths from past cultures. It is about making connections with people, with ideas, and with values. It is about communicating, and about inspiration. And what is so wonderful is that each of us can do it.

This book is about telling stories in the workplace. Librarians have a unique opportunity to learn from the growing body of literature regarding organizational storytelling. We are lovers of stories, but often we overlook the stories that are closest to us—our own stories, the stories of those with whom we work, and the stories of those we serve.

When I began to tell students about my experiences as a little girl in a wonderful public library children's department, I used it to launch a discussion of core values such as equity of access and intellectual freedom. In the workplace, the same story could be used to generate a brainstorming session about planning a redesign of children's services, the circulation workflow, or the latchkey children's policy. When we tell stories and, just as important, when we listen to the stories of those around us, things just seem to matter more. We enhance our understanding and form bonds. This, in turn, makes a better workplace, which makes happier and more creative workers and generates an ongoing cycle of quality improvement.

Welcome to *Organizational Storytelling for Librarians: Using Stories for Effective Leadership.* This book will help librarians understand new ways to use the skills we have developed, or perhaps left undeveloped, to communicate with each other and with our communities. I will share with you some of what I've learned about organizational storytelling from the key thinkers in this area, including David Boje, Stephen Denning, and Annette Simmons. Then I will look at some unique applications of organizational storytelling for libraries, from sharing values to building community. I will also relate examples I found through interviewing librarians who are excellent organizational storytellers. Those conversations were key in the development of my thinking about this topic and play an important part in the book. The last chapter will focus on building your own storytelling skills—including types of stories, stories that match specific situations, story triggers, and building your own organizational storytelling skills.

Note

1. Stephen Denning, "Storytelling for Organizational Change," in *The Springboard* (Boston: Butterworth-Heinemann, 2001), xiii–xxiii.

chapter one
STORYTELLING RETOOLED

Not everything that can be counted counts,
and not everything that counts can be counted.
—Albert Einstein

WHAT DO YOU think of when you hear the word *storytelling*? Chances are you typically think of something like Little Red Riding Hood, Anansi the Spider, or Peter Rabbit. We grew up with these stories. Libraries are by their very definitions repositories of stories, and many librarians tell stories as a key part of their jobs. We use stories with children to entertain, to teach, and to share culture. We understand the value of stories for children.

We are also surrounded by stories in daily life. When we wake up in the morning, we remember the stories in our dreams. We turn on the news or open the newspaper and hear stories of events and people beyond our front door. We look out our window and see elements of story everywhere—a woman feeding the squirrels, the young neighbor polishing her new car, the student walking to school with his heavy backpack. Once at work, we chat with friends and coworkers about the previous evening, the news, the upcoming day. And yet all these stories embedded in us and surrounding us typically have no legitimate place in our modern workday.

There are applications of storytelling beyond the children's services area in our libraries. Stories have great potential to inform, enlighten, persuade, and connect among adults as well as with children. Librarians are lovers of stories, but often we overlook the stories that are closest to us—our own stories, the stories of those with whom we work, and the stories of those we serve. Stories add richness to our lives and help us make sense of the world.

We have many opportunities to use stories in our daily work life. We can learn to *retool* storytelling, based on what we know to be true about stories and what we can learn anew about their potential in organizations, where stories can be shared for communication and community building. Organizational storytelling also involves *listening* to the stories of others—the people with whom we work, our patrons, and our funders. For librarians, there is no need to explain the value of storytelling. However, we can learn to bring storytelling out of the children's room and into our daily interactions with each other, our patrons, and our funders. We can learn to use the daily stories of our lives to enhance our organizational lives. Telling stories is essentially about sharing experiences and thus making connections with people, ideas, and values; *organizational storytelling* is about learning how to do that effectively in the workplace.

Organizational Storytelling

Although at the time I didn't see the explicit connection, I experienced an early realization of the communicative power of organizational storytelling when reading *The Social Life of Information* shortly after it was published in 2000.[1] This academic but quite readable book emphasizes the essential *human* quality of information as it is shared. *The Social Life of Information* is where I first read John Seely Brown's story of the Xerox Corporation's technician staff members, through whom research demonstrated the essential business value of shared coffee breaks. With time together over coffee, technicians could chat informally about their work. This sharing was significantly more effective for developing copier maintenance skills than the typical process charts or printed manuals. Research clearly demonstrated the greater economic value of employee sharing over closely regulated, quantifiable performance measures. This vignette was a "boring" example of organizational storytelling—after all, these were technicians, talking about the inner workings of photocopy machines—but in a sense the very dry content of those shared stories made the example even more powerful. It was the human shar-ing of common experience that brought power to the information, and that made it relevant to the teller and to the listener.

There is a second example of story in that book that has stuck with me for the decade since I read it and one that I use continually in my teaching. It's a story that coauthor Paul Duguid told about his experience in a closed-stacks archive, where he was reviewing 250-year-old primary documents for a research project. Duguid, who suffers from asthma, was careful to cover his nose and mouth with a scarf while working with the dusty documents. One day, a fellow researcher in the study room (to Duguid's horror, as he recalls it) spent his time with a box of letters not reading them, but instead holding each letter to his face, drawing deep breaths through his nose to capture its smell. Here's what Duguid writes about their conversation:

> Choking behind my mask, I asked him what he was doing. He was, he told me, a medical historian. (A profession to avoid if you have asthma.) He was documenting outbreaks of cholera. When that disease occurred in a town in the eighteenth century, all letters from that town were disinfected with vinegar to prevent the disease from spreading. By sniffing for the faint traces of vinegar that survived 250 years and noting the date and source of the letter, he was able to chart the progress of cholera outbreaks.[2]

I have used this story repeatedly when talking about digitization in libraries. It is a perfect illustration of the potential losses we face when we digitize—what information we lose when we move from physical to electronic and how we may be totally unaware and unsuspecting about those potential losses.

Although these two examples from *The Social Life of Information* are very different and are used to make different points, they are connected by their effective illustrations of the power of story. The first example shows the essential quality of human sharing within every workplace and for every job. Rather than the coffee break strictly being a "soft" investment for happy workers, structuring informal conversation in the workplace is also a sound business investment for knowledge management. The second example of the vinegar-scented primary documents shows the power of a simple story to illustrate a point, to facilitate learning, and to stick in one's memory over time. Quite frankly, I don't remember much else from *The Social Life of Information,* although it is on my bookshelf and I do still take it down and reread various sections. But I remember these two stories quite clearly and share them frequently.

These points about the power of story (the importance of human sharing in the workplace and the "stickiness"[3] of story) are made over and over in the emerging body of work on organizational storytelling. There is growing acknowledgment that our twentieth-century emphasis on mechanics, logic, and the quantitative should be revised in light of twenty-first-century social norms and behaviors. Remember Dagwood's workplace from the *Blondie* comic strip? That was an environment reflective of our twentieth-century paradigm: hierarchical, task-oriented, pretty boring, and governed by a patriarchal boss who could fire at will or on a whim.

Much has changed in the twenty-first-century workplace and for the twenty-first-century worker. Technology has facilitated greater connections, but much of that has been at the expense of lost human face-to-face interaction. We are awash with data, information, and connections, but we sometimes suffer from a lack of that human touch. As Annette Simmons puts it, "People float in an ocean of data and disconnected facts that overwhelm them with choices. . . . In this ocean of choice, a meaningful story can feel like a life preserver that tethers us to something safe, important, or at the very least more solid than disembodied voices begging for attention."[4] It's not just about *telling* stories in the workplace, but rather an acknowledgment and understanding of the deeper significance stories have in the role of community and basic human interaction. Stories explain, inspire, comfort, and in general help us understand the complexities of daily life in small and large ways.

Stories for Libraries, Stories for Leadership, and Stories for Building Community

Many people in the business community and from various academic disciplines are writing in the broad area of organizational narrative. There are applications in communications, social sciences, decision-making, and leadership, to name just a few. I will focus on three broad categories of organizational storytelling: stories for organizations (for our purposes, stories for libraries), stories for leadership, and stories for building community.

Stories for Libraries: The Organizational Narrative

I love to use literature in my teaching, and I do so as often as possible. For example, *Fahrenheit 451* and *1984* are excellent tools to stimulate deep thought and discussion when exploring issues of intellectual freedom, privacy, and information in a democracy. Josephine Tey's *The Daughter of Time* is another book I use when teaching about the information profession. It's a mystery novel about England's Richard III, exploring the unsolved murder of Richard's two young nephews, heirs to his throne. Was Richard III their murderer? Or was it his successor Henry VII? How much is historical fact, and how much of Richard's story do we believe based on accounts written by historians in the employ of the next king? (Hint: Henry Tudor, later Henry VII, defeated Richard in battle to ascend to the throne. Richard and Henry were not on friendly terms.) Whatever you believe about the death of the princes in the tower, *The Daughter of Time* is a book that makes a clear point: whoever controls the information gets to tell the story, and whoever gets to tell the story wins. This is true just as much in the workplace as it is in history. Learn to capture and even construct your own story, as well as your organization's story.

You can call this anything from "premise control"[5] to "spin" to "taking the bull by the horns," but basically the idea is that you want to control your own story and the story of your organization. First, you must be aware that there is a story out there, whether you are the one telling it or not!

Stories are among our earliest forms of communication. The ancient cave paintings, Greek and Roman myths, and biblical parables are all forms of stories that inform, teach, and inspire toward action. It is through these types of stories that cultural norms and modes of behavior are transmitted from generation to generation. So, too, are organizational behavior norms transmitted at work, through personal storytelling and through larger stories, sometimes referred to as "organizational narratives."

An organization is essentially a social system, made up of workers who come from a wide variety of backgrounds and belief systems. Karl Weick, a scholar in organizational theory, writes about the challenges of "sensemaking" within the contemporary organization.[6] One method of sensemaking is through the construction of an organizational narrative. A classic organizational narrative is described by David Boje as the BME (beginning, middle, and end) retrospective narrative.[7]

The BME narrative is just what it sounds like—a cohesive story about an organization from its origins to its current state, with the metaphorical "end" sometimes used as a vision narrative. Boje tells us that a good retrospective narrative is very important to an organization; it tells us all about the organization's (or in our case, the library's) mission and early days. It will include some heroes, such as the founding mothers and fathers whose ideas still guide us today. The narrative might also include some key events in the library's life, such as a successful censorship challenge or the construction of a new building. Memories of converting the card catalog to the OPAC would be in many of those library narratives. What else? Think about your own organization's narrative, or in other words, your library's life story. Who are the heroes of your library's story? What are some of the key events from your library's past, and how might you weave those into a compelling contemporary tale that will help you move forward?

Sylvia Jenkins is the vice president of academic affairs at Moraine Valley Community College. When I interviewed her for this book, she was Moraine Valley's dean of learning resources and academic development. In that role, she worked with librarians, library users, and faculty across the college. As the director of the library, Sylvia knew her organization's story and used it intentionally as she led (and continues to lead) toward the future.

> I tell new people as they come into the organization that even though we want to move forward, because that's what we're all about—advancing, improving, and moving forward—it's very important to know where you've come from in order to make that happen. I tell new faculty members especially that I believe that they are very fortunate to be able to work at a college like Moraine Valley, that it's a very forward-thinking, progressive school—but it didn't happen without hard work: hard work that was put in by other faculty members who came before them. It's important that they know about those faculty members—faculty members who didn't mind unpacking the boxes, and taking the desks out, and putting the computers on the desks. You know, those things didn't happen with them staying at home and dictating or delegating it to somebody else—you had to show up and do it. And the reason why I think it's important is that I want to impress upon them the expectations we have for them: yes, you've been hired to teach, and yes, you have a base load of classes that you have to teach—but making an organization what it is requires more than

that. It requires you participating, it requires you doing things outside of that fifteen credit-hour base load that you have. And if you want the organization to be what you think it should be, you have to participate.[8]

In the example above, Sylvia Jenkins uses the organizational narrative to communicate organizational values and to express cultural behavioral norms. I include more examples of this kind in chapter 2, which focuses on using organizational storytelling to communicate values and vision. You can also use an organizational narrative very effectively externally. Doing this well can be powerful marketing. Martha Hale's article "Stories in the Workplace" provides an excellent introduction to this idea for librarians. "Stories provide a human face to library advocacy, orientation, and discovery."[9] Think of a component of your own organizational narrative that you'd like to highlight and how you'd like to use it.

For example, say your academic library prides itself on its strong information literacy program. Could you use that internal pride to create an external marketing program, simply by telling your information literacy story more effectively? Get the students involved in creating a video, or write a short vignette about one person's experience in an information literacy session. Our stories evolve as we tell them and as more people get involved in the telling/listening/retelling process.

Stories for Leadership

Storytelling in the workplace can also be highly effective at this more personal level, particularly in the area of leadership. Much of the literature about organizational storytelling focuses on how leaders can learn to use stories more effectively to communicate. When thinking of leadership, by the way, include yourself, no matter what your position or job title in the library. Building leadership skills is something everyone should consider, because leadership comes from all across the organization.

Who I Am, and Why I Am Here

One of the best ways for a leader to connect to her audience is to share parts of herself: where she comes from, what brought her to this profession and this particular job, and what her values are. Sharing personal stories (both good ones and not-so-good ones) makes the leader more human. Chances are that parts of the leader's story will connect with the listeners. Two of Annette Simmons's "Six Stories You Need to Know How to Tell" are in this category: the "who I am" stories and the "why I am here" stories.[10] And as Simmons says, if you don't tell them these things, people will form their own assumptions and tell their stories about you. You can control what people think about who you are and why you are there simply by telling them—by sharing your story.

A wonderful example of this can be found in Danny Meyer's book *Setting the Table*.[11] In this memoir, Meyer tells his personal story about life as a restaurateur—from his early youthful inspirations to the current group of highly successful restaurants he owns and manages. Throughout the book Meyer talks about things he's proud of as well as some missteps he's made along the way; he highlights lessons learned through experience and through mentorship. The essence of Meyer's book, however, is not the field of restaurant management. His real focus is on customer service and community building, no matter what the field of endeavor. For this reason alone I would highly recommend the book to librarians. But in terms of storytelling, Meyer's book is also a wonderful illustration of the power of "who I am" and "why I am here" stories; in telling us his story, Meyer communicates to us his passion for food and for people, and we are inspired by his lessons. I have included some great examples of "who I am" and "why I am here" stories from the field of librarianship in this book, particularly where I talk about using stories to communicate values within our own organizations.[12]

Springboard Stories

Another early discovery I made in the realm of organizational storytelling was Stephen Denning's "springboard" story. Denning was an executive at the World Bank in the 1990s when he discovered the communicative potential of storytelling. He wanted to share his excitement about possible growth areas for the World Bank in the area of global knowledge sharing. This idea was not selling well at all, and Denning was struggling mightily to give life to the new concept. By chance, Denning started telling a brief vignette about a health worker in Zambia. That health worker was getting lifesaving information from a distant information source, via the Internet. But, as Denning told the story to key decision-makers, the World Bank, despite huge potential to facilitate information sharing in developing countries, *wasn't in* that Zambia success story. "*But what if it were?*" Denning asked.[13]

The brief story didn't have the typical story structure—no plot, no development, no real hero, and no clear ending. What it did provide was a springboard for the listener—the *"what if we were . . ."* that opened minds to new possibilities and gave each of those minds the freedom to imagine independently. Denning writes:

> A tiny story—29 words or 200 bytes—is less a vehicle for communication of large amounts of information and more a tiny fuse that ignites a new story in the listeners' minds, which establishes new connections and patterns in the listeners' existing information, attitudes, and perceptions.[14]

Using Stories to Persuade

Persuasion is an interesting concept. Sometimes it's about getting someone to accept a new idea, and sometimes it's about actually changing people's minds about a firmly held belief. ("That won't work here" could be a firmly held belief.) What persuades you to accept a new idea or to change your mind?

Many people would say that this is based on personality type; an individual makes decisions either through intuition or through logic, for example. But most people do a little of both, and so to base a proposal on logic makes good sense. This is of course what we have learned to do in the business world, where each proposal for a new idea must be supported with hard evidence from feasibility studies, statistics, and budget projections.

But more and more there is an acknowledgment that you must engage a listener's heart as well as his mind if you truly want to generate commitment for change or for a new idea. Stories pull the listener in and make individual human connections that data and information alone cannot make.

Confirmation Bias

Recently we have been hearing more about the concept of "confirmation bias," where a person tends to seek out information that confirms his or her established beliefs. In the information field, we have been worried about this from the perspective of "personal information filters"—where technology does indeed make it quite easy to receive very specialized packages of information based on a person's profiled interests and biases.

Stephen Denning reports on a 1979 study that actually demonstrates people's tendency to read information from their established perspective, and then to interpret that information as supporting their point of view.[15]

Subsequent research actually studied brain scans of research participants as they reviewed partisan political information. These scans showed—quite interestingly—very little activity from the parts of the brain associated with reasoning and increased activity in brain circuits connected to human emotion. As the experiment proceeded, data showed that the parts of the brain associated with rewards also became active once the participant found a way to match the information to an existing bias; the resulting pleasure sensors stimulated by the brain once again reinforced the original bias.

> The confirmation bias helps explain why the traditional approach of trying to persuade people by giving them reasons to change isn't a good idea if the audience is at all skeptical, cynical, or hostile. If a leader offers reasons at the outset of a communication to such an audience, the maneuver will likely activate the confirmation bias and the reasons for change will be reinterpreted as reasons not to change. This occurs without the thinking part of the brain being activated: the audience becomes even more deeply dug into its current contrary position. Reasons don't work at the outset, because the audience is neither listening nor thinking.[16]

What Denning proposes, then, is a three-step process: (1) get the audience's attention; (2) elicit desire for a different future; and (3) reinforce with reasons. Stories are effective at each of these stages.

1. Get the audience's attention.

Denning suggests a negative story here. Frequently your audience is not completely focused on your presentation; they may be daydreaming about lunch, grocery shopping, or piles of unfinished work. You want to grab their attention, and a negative story has been shown to be effective for this result. Denning suggests stories about the organization's or individuals' problems, and perhaps even how those problems are getting worse. Another option is to tell a story about adversity and possibly connect that adversity to a current situation.

2. Elicit desire for a different future.

Negative stories get attention, but they also generate worry and anxiety.[17] And while a negative story will grab the audience's attention, a positive story is more likely to inspire them to new action. These positive stories can be small or large, but most frequently they connect in some way to a similar problem in the past where there has been a positive outcome due to a new idea. For libraries, that might mean telling a story about how another library successfully moved to a team-based leadership model or successfully completed a bond initiative for increased library staffing and services.

3. Reinforce with reasons.

The last step in the process is to give the audience supporting data and information to confirm the need for a change. Even this stage of the process can be accomplished with stories. Denning suggests

- stories of what the change is, often seen through the eyes of some typical characters who will be affected by the change
- the story of how the change will be implemented, showing in simple steps how we will get from here to there
- the story of why the change will work, showing the underlying causal mechanisms that make the change virtually inevitable.[18]

This three-step process of getting the audience's attention, eliciting desire for a different future, and reinforcing with reasons is an excellent template for working with people rather than against them, engaging their emotions as well as their logic when it comes to leading toward a new vision. Emotions are not sufficient without logic, just as logic alone will not create passionate commitment to a new idea.

Chapter 3, "Using Stories to Navigate Change," will look more closely at using organizational storytelling to help facilitate change. Getting people to truly listen to you is the first step, and engaging their emotions is an essential part of this process.

Getting the Story Right

There is a caveat to all this. When using examples told through stories, it's essential that you get the story right. Beware of the heartwarming story that turns out to be not quite true or just a little off. Politicians often make this kind of mistake, and today's information technologies make disconfirmation quite easy. For example, Al Gore was burned by this in the 2000 presidential campaign, when he told the story of a young Florida girl in an overcrowded classroom. Gore hoped to generate support for his educational funding plans, but instead, due to some subtle but definite inaccuracies in his story, the whole thing backfired. See Denning's book *The Secret Language of Leadership* for an informative description of Gore's missteps in the area of storytelling, as well as how Gore eventually became a masterful storyteller in his work on global climate change.

The takeaway for us is the danger in telling a story poorly, or worse, a story that is inaccurate. Gore's inaccuracies were just enough to totally discredit his message, causing subsequent collateral damage way beyond the lost potential of that single story. The message actually becomes destructive to your cause, as your credibility is completely lost. Check your facts if you are using real stories about real people.

Reframing

Check your *frame* as well.[19] An effective way to present information is to reframe it, or see it from a different point of view. Each person comes to a situation with a backstory and with her own filters, and each person interprets a situation based on those filters. Frequently, a leader can frame a situation in a way that provides better control (or spin!) on an organizational event. An example of this comes from the book *The Art of Possibility:*

> A shoe factory sends two marketing scouts to a region of Africa to study the prospects for expanding business. One sends back a telegram saying: SITUATION HOPELESS STOP NO ONE WEARS SHOES. The other writes back triumphantly: GLORIOUS BUSINESS OPPORTUNITY STOP THEY HAVE NO SHOES. Each scout comes to the scene with his own perspective; each returns telling a different tale.[20]

Framing a story can be quite powerful; how we frame a story significantly affects how the content is received. This example shows how a subtle shift in perception and attitude can produce completely different results.

But again, beware of the inauthentic story or frame. Here's a pretty positive spin that might sound good, but would in truth be quite offensive:

> Several hundred happy passengers arrived safely in New York after the *Titanic*'s maiden voyage.

Stories for Building Community: Effective Listening

True influences come from knowing the listener's story. This holds true for the people inside the organization, as well as knowing your customers' stories. Consider a different point of view; walk in another's shoes. A powerful example is the story of Oz told from the "bad" witch's point of view; Gregory Maguire's novel *Wicked* helps us to see that there can be a whole new way of looking at something we took for granted. Listening to different points of view adds a sense of respect for the listeners, providing a deep acknowledgment of their value. And building connections through listening to others' stories truly builds community.

Professional storyteller Jack Maguire describes the "three Rs" of good listening:

- Remain silent until the other person has finished speaking.
- Respond with appropriate verbal and nonverbal cues.
- Remind yourself afterward of what you've heard that day.[21]

Stories have tremendous potential to connect us to each other. Sharing aspects of your own life with others, and truly listening to their stories as well, connects us to each other in powerful ways. It is important to create opportunities for sharing stories both within the organization and for your library's customers. Chapter 4 of this book focuses on the important topic of community building through storytelling. First, however, I will explore the potential of stories for sharing personal and organizational values in chapter 2 and using stories to help navigate change in chapter 3.

Notes

1. John Seely Brown and Paul Duguid, *The Social Life of Information* (Boston: Harvard Business School Press, 2000).
2. Ibid., 173–74.
3. "Stickiness" refers to the ability of an idea to remain vital over time. See, for example, *Made to Stick,* by Chip Heath and Dan Heath. The authors include "stories" as their sixth principle of a successful idea, or an idea that is "made to stick."
4. Annette Simmons, *Whoever Tells the Best Story Wins: How to Use Your Own Stories to Communicate with Power and Impact* (New York: American Management Association, 2007), 5.

5. Karl Weick, *Sensemaking in Organizations* (Thousand Oaks, CA: Sage, 1995), 170.

6. Weick describes "sensemaking" as a complex process that includes placing events within a context or framework, comprehending, and constructing meaning. See Weick, *Sensemaking in Organizations.*

7. David Boje, *Storytelling Organizations* (Thousand Oaks, CA: Sage, 2008), 9–11.

8. Sylvia Jenkins, interviewed by Kate Marek, July 7, 2009.

9. Martha Hale, "Stories in the Workplace," *Public Libraries* 42, no. 3 (May/June 2002): 166.

10. A complete list of Annette Simmons's "Six Stories You Need to Know How to Tell," from *The Story Factor,* can be found in chapter 6 of the present volume.

11. Danny Meyer, *Setting the Table: The Transforming Power of Hospitality in Business* (New York: HarperCollins, 2006).

12. See particularly chapter 2, "Communicating Vision and Values."

13. See chapter 3, "Using Stories to Navigate Change," for a more extensive discussion of springboard stories.

14. Stephen Denning, *The Springboard* (Boston: Butterworth-Heinemann, 2001), 82.

15. Stephen Denning, *The Secret Language of Leadership: How Leaders Inspire Action through Narrative* (San Francisco: John Wiley, 2007), 23–38.

16. Ibid., 26.

17. Ibid., 33.

18. Ibid., 36.

19. "Framing" an idea or issue puts a specific focus on one aspect of it, such as when you frame a particular aspect of a work of art. Adjusting your frame changes your perspective in some way, whether it be a subtle change or a broader one.

20. Rosamund Zander and Benjamin Zander, *The Art of Possibility* (New York: Penguin, 2002), 9.

21. Jack Maguire, *The Power of Personal Storytelling: Spinning Tales to Connect With Others* (New York: Jeremy P. Tarcher/Putnam, 1998), 231.

chapter two
COMMUNICATING VISION AND VALUES

Transmitting values is one of the trickier management challenges. . . .
Work can be dictated, but behavior only influenced.
—Stephen Denning

IN HIS CLASSIC book *The Fifth Discipline,* Peter Senge stresses the importance of a shared vision to a learning organization. Here's a story Senge uses to illustrate shared vision:

> You may remember the movie *Spartacus,* an adaptation of the story of a Roman gladiator/slave who led an army of slaves in an uprising in 71 B.C. They defeated the Roman legions twice, but were finally conquered by the general Marcus Crassus after a long siege and battle. In the movie, Crassus tells the thousand survivors in Spartacus's army, "You have been slaves. You will be slaves again. But you will be spared your rightful punishment of crucifixion by the mercy of the Roman legions. All you need to do is turn over to me the slave Spartacus, because we do not know him by sight."
>
> After a long pause, Spartacus (played by Kirk Douglas) stands up and says, "I am Spartacus." Then the man next to him stands up and says, "I am Spartacus." The next man stands up and also says, "No, I am Spartacus." Within a minute, everyone in the army is on his feet.[1]

The slaves, Senge says, held a single shared vision: freedom from slavery. Although their bond to Spartacus was strong, ultimately their passionate allegiance was to the vision he inspired rather than to the individual man. By standing up, each man chose death rather than the loss of that vision. Senge calls a shared vision "a force in people's hearts, a force of impressive power."[2]

Within the concept of "shared vision," there is an explicit implication of shared values. Whether the shared value is at a company such as Walmart with Sam Walton's original value to be the people's store, a company such as Southwest Airlines where the values speak to service with fun, or a library's shared values of universal citizen access to information, shared values within an organization lay the groundwork for a shared vision and provide tremendous power.

In libraries, we have a head start on this concept of shared values. Librarians share the legacy of being stewards of the human record. In Western democracies, we have a system of government based on universal citizen participation, with informed decision-making essential to the process. Universal access to information, without fear of censure, is a value that firmly took hold in American library culture in the twentieth century. Other values shared in the library profession include equity of access to information, barrier-free information environments, information privacy, lifelong learning, and service to the user.

Unfortunately, in library organizations we sometimes forget the power of these shared values. Librarians and library administrators who can communicate those values across the organization have a unique potential to inspire action and build community. Connecting people to shared values, and then giving people a stake in the organization based on those values, results in new energy across the library. We can begin to ask, as Peter Block encourages us, "What can we create together?"[3]

Using Stories to Communicate Organizational Values

One of the most compelling accounts I've read of the exceptional potential of story to communicate organizational values is the concept of the "sacred bundle."[4] Building from the concept of the BME narrative described in chapter 1, the sacred bundle is a collection of special events and heroic acts in an organization's history. It is the essential bits of "who we are" that we depend on in the present and carry forward into the future. Listen to this account of the sacred bundle as told by consultant and author Peg Neuhauser:

> Organizational consultant Ray Sells tells about the time that he was taking a tour of the Chicago Museum of History and came across an exhibit about the Plains Indians of North America. One of the items in that exhibit caught his attention. It was described as a "sacred bundle." This was a bundle of hides containing items that look like a collection of odds and ends. According to Ray, the items could easily have been mistaken for debris. There was a feather, some rocks, an old peace pipe, an eagle's claw, and a few worn pouches. The description that accompanied the exhibit explained that this bundle contained the historical and sacred mementos of this particular tribe. It was entrusted to one of the elders of the tribe, and that person was expected to protect the sacred bundle with his life, if necessary. To lose the sacred bundle would threaten the tribal identity for the entire group.[5]

The sacred bundle stories represent the story of an organization—its heart and soul, according to Neuhauser—and provide a mechanism for its culture to survive in times of change. The sacred bundle lays the foundation for Senge's shared vision, and together they help create a single emotional connection within each person to the roots and meaning of the organization.

Teaching about the sacred bundle is a fundamental mechanism for building and sustaining a strong organization, and it is a key role of leadership. By telling and retelling sacred bundle stories, a leader can create continuity, send messages, and build a strong organizational culture. It is through knowledge of the sacred bundle that we learn who we are, where we came from, and where we are headed.

It is also important to make sure all members of the organization are included around this metaphorical campfire where stories are told. Sharing these sacred stories with only an elite few within an organization is counterproductive; just as Spartacus's entire army understood why they were fighting, all members of the organization need to understand its roots and values. I am amazed that oftentimes in libraries, frontline staff members such as circulation clerks don't "know about" the core values of the information profession—democratic values mentioned earlier such as equity of access to information, intellectual freedom, and individual patron privacy. How can we expect our frontline employees to be mindful of patron privacy if they don't recognize it as a feather from our sacred bundle?

Library Examples

Here are two compelling examples of library leaders who build organizational culture through sacred bundle stories.

Sylvia Jenkins
Moraine Valley Community College (Palos Hills, Illinois)

When she was dean of both the library and of the campus academic development department, Sylvia Jenkins of Moraine Valley Community College wore many hats. She is a master storyteller and truly understands how to use stories effectively. Part of the organizational value system that Sylvia intentionally communicates to new employees is the concept of shared ownership, and thus shared responsibility, for the teaching and learning organization as a whole. I first used this story in chapter 1 when talking about sharing the organizational narrative; read it this time from the perspective of communicating shared organizational values.

> I tell new people as they come into the organization that even though we want to move forward, because that's what we're all about—advancing, improving, and moving forward—it's very important to know where you've come from in order to make that happen. I tell new faculty members especially that I believe that they are very fortunate to be able to work at a college like Moraine Valley, that it's a very forward-thinking, progressive school—but it didn't happen without hard work. Hard work that was put in by other faculty members who came before them. It's important that they know about those faculty members—faculty members who didn't mind unpacking the boxes, and taking the desks out, and putting the computers on the desks. You know, those things didn't happen with them staying at home and dictating or delegating it to somebody else. You had to show up and do it. [I think it's important to share this because] I want to impress upon them the expectations we have for them—that yes, you've been hired to teach, and yes, you have a base load of classes that you

> have to teach—but making an organization what it is requires more than that. It requires you participating, it requires you doing things outside of that fifteen credit-hour base load that you have. And if you want the organization to be what you think it should be, you have to participate.[6]

Sylvia weaves her life experience into the story of the community college, effectively sharing her own priorities as a leader as well as her sense of the organization's key values.

Carolyn Anthony
Skokie Public Library (Skokie, Illinois)

Another library leader who uses stories effectively in her leadership is Carolyn Anthony, director of the Skokie (Illinois) Public Library. Carolyn captures and uses stories from the community, turning them into what she calls "viral stories." Viral stories gain power as they are told and retold; part of the power of the story comes from its shared ownership. Here's an example of a story that demonstrates several things from the Skokie Public Library's sacred bundle: its legacy and continuity of service to the community, the potential of the library to impact an individual's life, and the power of lifelong learning offered through the library's programs and resources.

Carolyn tells this story of a simple expression of thanks from a library user; through Carolyn's telling the story went "viral" and was heard far beyond the Skokie community.

> I remember a Skokie Public Library event celebrating fifty years of a Great Books discussion group. An elderly woman attended the event; she came in slowly, using a walker. The woman, who had attended the Great Books discussion groups since she was young, told her own story of the program's impact on her life. "My parents couldn't afford to send me to college, and this book group became my college."
>
> I was so moved by this story that I retold it at a conference presentation I made shortly thereafter. Later that day, I dropped by the Great Books Foundation booth, and they had already heard the story I had told![7]

Many of us no doubt have heard countless inspiring stories from our library customers and community members. Using those stories effectively gives them life beyond our own buildings and creates an impact on feelings, memories, and beliefs.

The Skokie Public Library is also known for its early response to the USA PATRIOT Act, passed by Congress shortly after the 9/11 terrorist attacks. Many libraries reacted against the PATRIOT Act's loosening of patron privacy protections we enjoy through our constitutional rights. As director, Carolyn Anthony was particularly active in the library community on this issue, making frequent appearances on discussion panels, radio interviews, and in other public debates about the PATRIOT Act. Skokie itself is a unique community in regard to its attitudes toward intellectual freedom, because its demographic mix includes many people who have previously lived, or whose parents lived, in totalitarian regimes. Skokie is also the home of the Illinois Holocaust Museum and Education Center. There is a strong emphasis on civil rights throughout the community. Through this combined visibility of the community and the library, Carolyn Anthony found herself in a national spotlight when it came to the library profession's response to the USA PATRIOT Act. It was through sharing the stories of members of her community that Carolyn was able to convey the importance of open access to information in a time of political fear. Stories of the Skokie Public Library's post-9/11 response have become a part of their sacred bundle, helping to communicate the library's values and organizational priorities.

Personal Values

Although the sacred bundle stories focus specifically on organizational values, storytelling is equally as valuable for communicating personal values such as honesty, integrity, and ethical conduct. A leader can talk about expectations of behavior in the workplace by using personal stories, parables, stories about heroes, fables, and more. Stories that reveal something about a leader's own personal values would be included in what Annette Simmons calls "who I am" stories, giving the listener an opportunity to learn more about the leader and her key influences.

A good illustration of this is another story from Sylvia Jenkins. By talking about her awareness of being helped throughout her own life, and her resulting commitment to live a life helping others, we come to know more not only about Sylvia herself, but about the personal value she places on a life of service. Whether or not workers in her institution also have individual commitments to lives of service, it is evident to everyone exactly what the boss expects and why. Her personal values influence the organizational values, and we can see the big picture quite clearly.

> When I went to undergraduate school at Grambling, . . . I ended up in situations where I had very nurturing faculty members, people who cared about me. And I grew up in a family that cared about me. I had obstacles I didn't even know I had, but because of the nurturing environment, and because of the strong will of my family and people I encountered, [I was able to succeed].
>
> If it wasn't for somebody else who turned around and helped me, I might not be where I am today. And if most of us think about our lives, regardless of how privileged you perceive you were, or how underprivileged you perceive you were, somebody somewhere along the way helped you to get to where you are. So what I ask of people is just take that time and think about that, and even if it means going that extra mile for that student who may not be there yet, what can you do differently to maybe pull that person in?[8]

This theme of the power of one person to help another person overcome educational and professional obstacles is an important one in Sylvia's leadership. She communicates this without preaching to her staff about customer service or positive attitudes, but by telling her own story of the doors others opened for her when she was young and vulnerable. Powerful indeed.

Like Sylvia, Carolyn Anthony often tells others about her own professional path and how her early experiences influenced her emerging professional values. Her own early experiences at the Enoch Pratt Free Library in Baltimore inspired her to spend her professional life building community partnerships, a passion she continues in Skokie. And, like Sylvia, Carolyn shares her own stories with new librarians, both inside and outside of her library. She sees the value of encouragement from a leader and the opportunities that encouragement brings to a young professional. Carolyn talks about the strong value she places on community partnerships by telling her own story rather than by preaching, or by instructing her staff in a more command-centered manner. She encourages new professionals to take advantage of personal and professional opportunities and to find their passion along the way. She draws on a favorite Quaker saying, "Let the way unfold . . . ," as she shares the story of her own still-unfolding path.

Telling your own personal story with honesty and humility, especially in terms of things you have learned along the way, opens you up to connections with others and at the same time provides a unique mechanism for them to understand your values and priorities. Talking about values through narrative also allows each individual listener the chance to understand the story within his own unique context, making those personal connections through individual reflection.

If, however, you are not comfortable talking about yourself, you can still use stories to share information about values. Library culture frequently includes familiarity with fables, folk tales, myths, and both classic and contemporary literary characters. Selecting specific parables or myths to retell will help communicate certain values; even dropping a well-known literary character's name can communicate your thinking.

Talk about your heroes (Eleanor Roosevelt, Abraham Lincoln, Rosa Parks, for example) and how they inspire you. Or talk about what you're reading. The point is to get out to the watercooler and share stories about things that are important to you, and to listen to the stories of others.

Author Peg Neuhauser encourages us to think about these things as we think about using stories effectively:

- What do you want listeners to feel?
- What do you want listeners to remember?
- What do you want listeners to believe?[9]

All of the examples here illustrate those ideas beautifully—the power of creating strong feelings, memories, and beliefs through sharing stories about our personal experiences and values.

Espoused Values versus Values-in-Action

Annette Simmons includes "values-in-action" stories as one of the types of stories all leaders need to know how to tell. Although experience is the best teacher, Simmons says that relating a story about an experience provides a useful alternative to the real thing. Opinions differ about the appropriate tone of a values-in-action story; Denning cautions against being moralistic or preachy, while other storytellers like to make a point of the "moral of the story."

David Armstrong, for example, is explicit with each story he tells in the workplace. His *Managing by Storying Around* is a collection of short vignettes, each with a very specific values message that comes as a stated part of the story. For example, Armstrong relates the story of a union shop where the management was struggling with issues of habitual tardiness by some employees. At the same time, the management was trying to move toward an environment of greater trust. Rather than continuing to bicker with the union over minutes clocked, the management instead decided to remove the time clock completely. The end result was positive all around; employees felt trusted and reacted with greater commitment, and the on-time rate improved dramatically. Armstrong lists five "morals" of that story, including "delegate," "listen," and "treat people like people."[10]

Another way to get to the point of the story with perhaps a little less moralizing (if you prefer) would be to end the story with one of the following options: "and this is what it meant to me," "this is what I learned from that experience," or "this is how my decisions have been influenced since that happened to me."[11]

A caveat: once again, personal stories used to illustrate values must be authentic. It is important to reinforce stories with action, demonstrating a strong connection between *espoused values* and true *values-in-action*. It is no use, for example, to say your hero is Abraham Lincoln because of his honesty, if you are known for using your keys to help yourself to free soft drinks from the staff room's pop machine.

At an organizational level, it can be quite damaging to have your espoused values be in conflict with your values-in-action. What if, for example, your mission statement includes a reference to "equity of access," but your circulation policy requires a picture ID and three official pieces of mail at a current address in order to obtain a library card? Your espoused value states inclusivity, but your value-in-action is exclusivity. Just one story about a family who couldn't get a library card because of your restrictive policies can go viral and will do significant damage to your reputation. That story will have much more power in the community than all your written statements about the value you place on equity.

Finding and Building Stories

It is easy to overlook the first step in creating values narratives: defining what you consider important. When thinking about your organization, what do you think belongs in your sacred bundle? How will you communicate that? And, from a personal perspective, what information about your own value system do you most want to convey? Defining important values takes a thoughtful process of reflection and introspection, at both the organizational and personal levels.

Building Sacred Bundle Stories

Defining events, persons, and artifacts in the library's history to include in your sacred bundle would be a wonderful exercise for a library staff day, a board retreat, or an executive leaders' session. This could be a preliminary event to planning, or it could stand alone as a unique celebration.

The following are some key questions to consider when building your sacred bundle stories.

1. What are five to ten pivotal events in your library's history?
   Depending on how old your library is, there will be key events such as its creation story, the story of its buildings, and stories of community events. Long-term projects such as the move from card catalog to OPAC should be included, along with anniversaries, awards, expansions or renovations, and ambitious long-range plans.

2. Who are your library's heroes?
   Everyone has heroes. Maybe these come from your public library board, your academic library's college leadership, your community, or your staff. Sometimes the library heroes are well known to today's staff, as their stories continue to be told. But do you have some heroes from years past whose stories should be dusted off and brought back to light? What was it about those persons that made them heroes? Remembering key people, and how they were significant in the life of the library, helps to highlight values that carry forward to today. It also brings people closer together through a sense of common parentage.

Here are a few examples of actual librarians who were heroes in their own libraries. As you read each example, think of the values that could be celebrated today by remembering these heroes.

- In his twenty-five years on the job, the director of a small liberal arts college library inspired more than fifteen students to become librarians and go to library school. After his retirement, the state library association established a library school scholarship in his name.
- A public library director in a small town in the Southwest led a pre–World War II fight to integrate the children's story hours. Because of her controversial stand on civil rights, the librarian was ultimately fired, but her impact is still remembered.
- A group of determined staff members rallied to reopen the library in a new location after a devastating fire wiped out half of the collection and destroyed the building.

3. What key values or characteristics of your library are highlighted in your stories?

If your library is well known for its lifelong learning programs, for community partnerships, or for its outstanding collections, make sure your library stories reflect those strengths.

Here is an example. A university librarian loves to tell sometimes humorous stories about designing the new library building, particularly ones regarding the committee that met for two years before construction began. The committee members, which included the university president, argued quite a bit about the design of the building but ultimately chose a floor plan that reflected a true sensitivity to twenty-first-century learners and information needs. In telling these stories, the university librarian celebrates the institutional commitment, from the president on down, to the library as a vital part of the university learning environment.

This is actually a great story example for another reason. The university librarian could choose to tell these stories from the point of view of tedious committee work, when reaching agreement was a slow, arduous process. She might even disparage certain specific committee members. Alternatively, choosing to tell the stories from a positive point of view, highlighting specific key values demonstrated by the university's commitment to an important new library building, can be a strategic choice for a positive future.

4. What physical objects or artifacts might you include in your sacred bundle?

   Consider what you might put in a cornerstone if you were erecting a new library building or celebrating a centennial. These kinds of artifacts should also be celebrated in full view of existing staff and customers. Things like photographs of important events and people, along with historical letters, can be framed and put in a visible, high-traffic area or a special memorial wall. Each library has a unique history, so these physical objects will be different for every library, but by thoughtfully selecting them and making them a part of your sacred bundle, you can help tell the story with more power and meaning.

5. What crisis events or stories are in your sacred bundle?

   How you remember crisis is important. Something significant such as a natural disaster (fire, earthquake, flood) can be an extremely difficult emotional memory for the staff and the community. Other examples of crisis could include a significant censorship challenge, the illness and loss of a beloved staff member, or the loss of significant administrative support through funding cuts or new governance. Recalling tough times through memory and story helps continue that common thread of organizational experience. Remember to incorporate a positive ending, if possible; times get tough, but the library pulls together and stays strong.

Building Personal Values Stories

The process of building personal values stories is very similar to constructing sacred bundle stories. Again, it involves examination and reflection. What do you want to communicate to your listeners? Think about those sacred bundle stories and apply them to your own experiences.

- What were some pivotal events in your life?
- Who are your heroes? What about library heroes?
- What important artifacts or objects do you treasure, and why?
- What crisis events in your life helped shape who you are today?

Here are some additional "story triggers" that might help you construct some personal values stories:

- What was one of your happiest days at work?
- What makes you proud to work in a library?
- How did you at one point in your life resolve a conflict between two values? (One option for this particular exercise is to consider the value conflict between pragmatism and idealism in library services.)

The more you begin to share your personal and organizational values through stories, the greater connections you can begin to build within your library. You will build trust, which leads to greater confidence and energy among people. When people feel safe, they are more likely to be creative, to share innovative ideas, and to build strong relationships.

It's also critical to listen to the stories of others. You can learn to be a better storyteller by paying attention to the stories you like best from other people. More important, however, it is through listening that you can complete the circle of connection that you begin by sharing your own story. It's the combination of sharing and listening that creates true communication.

Shared Values to Shared Vision

The story of Spartacus and his army illustrates the power of shared values and the resulting ability to create a shared vision. The soldiers in Spartacus's army were deeply attached to their common purpose. Gathering and sharing sacred bundle stories can help create those deep attachments to the library's mission, and sharing personal values stories can create individual connections toward a cohesive staff.

In the next two chapters, I will look more closely at the concepts of "change" and "community," extending the potential of stories and shared experience into the broader library context.

Notes

1. Peter Senge, *The Fifth Discipline: The Art and Practice of the Learning Organization* (New York: Doubleday, 1990), 205.
2. Ibid., 206.

3. See chapter 4 for a more focused look at Peter Block's work.
4. Peg Neuhauser, *Corporate Legends and Lore* (Austin, TX: PCN Associates, 1993), 42.
5. Ibid.
6. Sylvia Jenkins, interviewed by Kate Marek, July 7, 2009.
7. Carolyn Anthony, interviewed by Kate Marek, August 13, 2009.
8. Sylvia Jenkins, interviewed by Kate Marek, July 7, 2009.
9. Neuhauser, *Corporate Legends and Lore,* 28.
10. David M. Armstrong, *Managing by Storying Around: A New Method of Leadership* (New York: Armstrong International, 1999), 17–18.
11. Stephen Denning, *The Leader's Guide to Storytelling* (San Francisco: Jossey-Bass, 2005), 138.

chapter three
USING STORIES TO NAVIGATE CHANGE

Being right doesn't mean people will listen to you.
—Annette Simmons

IMAGINE YOU ARE a white-water rafter. This sport involves the thrill of navigating your small raft, which you and your partners control, through rushing river waters full of twists, turns, swirls, and unexpected wave crashes. With close attention, skill, strength, and teamwork you can come through the river white water within a few short minutes, relax your attention, and congratulate each other on a thrilling and successful ride. Then you enjoy the calm and beauty of the river. You have reached a stable state. You know the next rapid is coming up ahead, but you have time to reflect on the previous challenge and prepare for the next.

Today we have lost the comfort of the stable state between white-water experiences; we live in a state of constant white water.[1] And yet it is human nature to crave the stable state—the comfort of knowing you have a home and a job in a peaceful, democratic country. Those of us in librarianship tend to love the stability of our profession, the core values of information services, and our role in educating citizens in a democracy. Even the phrase "I am a librarian" indicates an internal acknowledgment of our unique identity and the stability of our profession. We were drawn to a legacy profession that has played a key role in the stable state, and yet our profession is truly in the midst of ongoing turbulent change.

How can we reconcile our life in constant white water with our human tendency to crave stability? What is it that helps makes people feel open to change? Business pragmatism would tell us to gather data, share statistics, and create a strategic plan. But what many change management experts have discovered is that it is not effective to try to convince people intellectually of the need for organizational change. Rather, we must change their feelings. We must touch their hearts rather than their minds, inspiring rather than directing, to get true buy-in and alter people's behavior. John Kotter, the highly regarded expert in change leadership, makes an essential point about leading people through change: "People change what they do less because they are given *analysis* that shifts their *thinking* than because they are *shown* a truth that influences their *feelings*."[2] Stories are a wonderful way to show people truths, and to touch their hearts in the process.

Creating a Sense of Urgency: Kotter's See-Feel-Change Model versus the Analyze-Think-Change Model

Emotion is not the only element in the formula to change people's minds. There is a role for both data and example, and even persons who are readily influenced by a story will have their opinions reinforced by supporting statistics or budget figures. But it's the story they will remember, and it's their emotional reaction that will stir them to action. In his extensive research, Kotter has found that "people changed less because of facts or data that shifted their thinking than because compelling experiences changed their feelings. This emotional component was always present in the most successful change stories and almost always missing in the least successful. Too many people were working on the mind without paying attention to the heart."[3] Communicating a compelling story is a key role of the leader who is paying attention to the hearts of those being led through change.

Kotter describes a core pattern revealed through his research on successful change:

1. See.
There is a general sense in the organization of a need for change or of a trouble spot. The leader should generate a striking situation or story that enables

the workers to clearly visualize the problem or to face its reality.

> LIBRARY EXAMPLE: The parents of a Hispanic schoolboy don't have the requisite photo IDs that the library rules require for borrowing privileges. The library director, knowing that a rule change in the abstract would not go over well with her longtime circulation manager, wants to change the language of the borrowing policy. To start the process, she finds out more about the Hispanic family and weaves their story into a description of the emerging needs of the community with regard to many new families in it. This way, they can all begin *to understand more about the patron's story.*

2. Feel.

Seeing the personal side of the rule's impact will awaken new feelings of understanding about the need for change and help create a sense of urgency for solving the problem.

> LIBRARY EXAMPLE: The circulation manager begins to feel the personal impact of the borrowing policies within the context of the library's changing community demographics. Connecting the policy to the limitations they impose on a real patron helps create an awareness of the need for change, along with a sense of ownership in moving the change forward for the sake of this family and others like them.

3. Change.

The new feelings change behavior or reinforce new behaviors. People are less complacent, try harder, and work more consciously toward the long-term goal.

> LIBRARY EXAMPLE: The circulation manager develops a new sensitivity to the patrons, going beyond his old focus on the rules. His new behaviors provide a model for the members of his department, and the new sensitivity spreads or is reinforced.

This library scenario developed to illustrate Kotter's core pattern of "see-feel-change" may seem slightly simplistic. But too often library department heads become separated from the customers they serve. No matter what type of library, the frontline staff workers are the ones who frequently have their fingers on the pulse of the community. Directors are privy to the big picture, including things such as evidence of demographic shifts. Middle managers must make a special effort to come face-to-face with the library patrons, bringing the customers' stories into all levels of the library. In the same way, frontline staff need to listen to the big picture and work to implement the library's mission in their face-to-face contacts with patrons.

Kotter's see-feel-change model of getting buy-in for change is closely paralleled by the multistage process recommended by Stephen Denning and mentioned earlier in chapter 1. Denning calls this process "key steps in the language of leadership." The steps are listed again here, this time using a specific library scenario to illustrate how stories can be incorporated into this process.

1. Getting the audience's attention.

The audience must be listening. Messages that are most likely to be attention-getting are personalized, evoke an emotional response, come from a trusted sender, and are concise. Some of the tools Denning suggests are to tell a story about the audience's problems; tell a story about how you (as the leader or speaker) handled adversity; ask a question; or use a striking metaphor.

> **LIBRARY EXAMPLE:** In an all-staff meeting day, the director of the Greenville Public Library starts her speech by telling the story of the young schoolboy whose parents cannot get a library card because they lack the proper identification. She uses his first name and includes parts of her conversations with the parents in the story. In telling the story, she does not focus on the outdated circulation policies as the problem, but instead frames the issue differently: the library is not adequately serving its customers.

2. Eliciting desire for a different future.

Denning says that the negative story that gets people's attention is much less effective in getting them to want to change their behavior. Here the emotional connection is essential. Denning also says the new idea must be worthwhile for its own sake, your communication tool must make the idea memorable, and the audience must be able to participate by making the idea their own. The story must be positive. Some tools Denning suggests are a demonstration or video of the idea or the suggested change in use; a positive, real-life story of the idea in use; the telling of a common memory story; or offering a positive challenge.

> LIBRARY EXAMPLE: The library director asks the youth services manager to recruit young adults in the creation of a short documentary about the problems faced by the local immigrant population. The library will partner with the local high school's social studies, civics, and journalism teachers, as well as the high school librarian. The completed film will be shown at the staff day, following the director's speech. At the end of the film, the library director again references the need for outreach to the full community.

3. Reinforcing with reasons.

Although the mental door is open to the idea of change, step in to offer supporting reasons for that change. This sequence of eliciting desire and then reinforcing with reasons is much more effective than the standard Western intellectual tradition of offering data before that emotional connection is made. A clear rationale with supporting documentation helps sustain the commitment to change. Denning suggests using data and statistics in context and using plausible stories that explain what the change is, how it will work, and how it will be executed.

> LIBRARY EXAMPLE: At this point, the library director in our scenario can introduce statistics about the number of community residents who are not being served by the library. She can include a "common memory" story about the library's commitment to education and lifelong literacy, matching the need for change to the library's mission and to broader professional ideals. A sacred bundle story would also work well here, one that recalls historical examples of outreach to new populations. In addition, the director can include a specific road map for an outreach program, with projections about the statistical impact of that program on the community within twelve months, weaving in a reference back to the characters in her original story.

4. Continuing the conversation.

Denning warns against internal entropy, a possible loss of focus, and potential dangers from the outside such as political backlash or unexpected budget changes. Denning suggests an ongoing organizational conversation to counteract these challenges; the conversation should include an openness to questions, as well as an active sharing of stories from staff and from customers.

> **LIBRARY EXAMPLE:** The end of the library director's speech is just the beginning of the change initiative toward diversity outreach. She wraps up the presentation with information about her own open-door policy, as well as new communication structures to keep the conversation flowing. She emphasizes her knowledge of each staff member's role in providing the best possible library service and welcomes ideas about how to best make that happen. Finally, she could introduce a story collection project that highlights small individual success stories from the community.

This very explicit pattern of events increases the already strong potential of narrative as a tool for effective change management. As you begin to think more about using stories for this purpose, it's helpful to expand your repertoire. The following section outlines several different kinds of stories, or story genres, that offer a range of tools for managing organizational change.

Specific Types of Stories Effective for Change Management: Real-Life Stories, Cautionary Tales, Business Fables, and Springboard Stories

Real-Life Stories

John Kotter is known for his work on leadership and on effective change management rather than organizational storytelling. However, we can find numerous examples of his use of story to illustrate his research. For example, his book *The Heart of Change,* cowritten with Dan Cohen, is essentially a collection of real leaders' experiences that illustrate Kotter's eight steps of effective change management. These real-life stories illustrate the power of Kotter's see-feel-change theory of effective communication, as opposed to an analyze-think-change approach.[4]

The earlier library scenario of circulation policies that needed revision in response to new immigrant populations in the community is an example of a real-life story. After the completion of any particular aspect of the change, the story can be used to sustain interest in the project. Simply communicating with the community is an example of telling the story. Here's how it might sound as a real-life story as told by the director through the library's newsletter or website:

> Here at Greenville Public Library, we have always prided ourselves on strong service to our community. A key part of our mission is lifelong education; my own great-grandparents were Italian immigrants who learned English through the help of the library's outreach programs. My grandfather, their oldest son, went on to be a library board member, and his stories inspired me to become a librarian. Now we have another growing immigrant population, this time Hispanic. But we have discovered that some of our current practices are actually preventing us from serving new families in our community. In conversation with the board and with library staff, the Greenville Public Library is developing a new outreach program that will include partnerships with Hispanic community organizations and the area literacy council. Please join us by sharing your ideas and your stories!

This story provides some elements of a legacy story as well as basic information about a future projection of the library's mission. (It also provides elements of Simmons's "who I am" and "why I am here" leadership stories, as described in chapter 1.) As the program develops, the story will also gain dimension and will become a part of "continuing the conversation."

Cautionary Tales

When I first read Karl Weick's 1996 *Administrative Science Quarterly* article "Drop Your Tools: An Allegory for Organizational Studies," I was struck by his powerful retelling of two historical events as an organizational cautionary tale.[5] The story focuses on two separate groups of firefighters who, in the face of rapidly escalating forest fires, disregarded instructions to drop their heavy tools and run. Tragically, in both instances this inability to drop the tools of their trade prevented the firefighters from gaining the essential time needed to outrun the fires. Many simply did not get out in time.

> The first of the two disasters, Mann Gulch . . . occurred on August 5, 1949, when 14 young smokejumpers, their foreman Wagner Dodge, and a forest ranger were trapped near the bottom of a 76-percent slope in western Montana by an exploding fire. Thirteen of these men were killed when they tried to outrun the fire, ignoring both an order to drop their heavy tools and an order to lie down in an area where fuel had been burned off by an escape fire. . . . At South Canyon, outside Glenwood Springs, Colorado, roughly the same thing happened 45 years later on July 6, 1994. Again, late on a hot, dry, windy afternoon, near 4:00 P.M., flames on the side of a gulch away from the firefighters jumped across onto their side beneath them. . . . Within seconds a wall of flame raced up the hill toward the firefighters on the west flank fireline. Failing to outrun the flames, 12 firefighters perished. Two helitack crew members on the top of the ridge also died when they tried to outrun the fire to the northwest.
>
> In both cases, the 23 men and four women were overrun by exploding fires when their retreat was slowed because they failed to drop the heavy tools they were carrying. By keeping their tools, they lost valuable distance they could have covered more quickly if they had been lighter. All 27 perished within sight of safe areas. The question is, why did the firefighters keep their tools?[6]

When under stress, people revert to what they know best, namely their familiar tools. But this behavior can be dangerous, and indeed lifethreatening. Weick's use of the firefighters' story is a powerful cautionary tale about what can happen to individuals, organizations, and professions if they are unable to hear external signals and make nimble changes to traditional work practices. It has a great deal of relevance for libraries and librarians in today's changing information environment. I have used it in my own work and in my teaching.[7]

Fear vs. Inspiration

Many experts who write about managing change, however, caution against the limited effectiveness of using fear to change behaviors over the long term. Fear often makes people freeze, retreat, or fight. What is needed instead is a call to action based on a shared understanding of a potential successful future, which may indeed include avoiding a death by inaction. For example, John Kotter emphasizes creating a sense of urgency as his first of eight steps for successful change.[8]

How can stories assist with creating a sense of urgency? Real stories such as the Drop Your Tools cautionary tale, and fictional stories such as John Kotter and Holger Rathgeber's *Our Iceberg Is Melting,* can both be used effectively to inspire action toward change.[9]

Business Fables

Our Iceberg Is Melting falls into the "business fable" literary genre, along with other stories such as *Who Stole My Cheese?* and *Squirrel, Inc.* In *Our Iceberg Is Melting,* a group of penguins in Antarctica is forced to consider leaving their home of many generations when one penguin discovers some disturbing evidence about the iceberg. The story illustrates how the group goes through Kotter's eight stages of effective change management, ending with the group successfully moving to a new home. With penguins as main characters, we can read the story as a much less threatening scenario. However, the personification in the writing, and the parallels between the dramatic changes the penguins face and our own constant white water, make the story an extremely effective vehicle for discussion and learning.

Springboard Stories

Stephen Denning calls stories that spark action "springboard" stories. His book *The Springboard: How Storytelling Ignites Action in Knowledge-Era Organizations* introduces the concept of this very specific genre, which can be used to open minds to new possibilities. "By a springboard story, I mean a story that enables a leap in understanding by the audience so as to grasp how an organization or community or complex system may change."[10]

For Denning, the complex system that needed changing was the World Bank of the early 1990s. The bank, historically a lending organization, was on the verge of stagnation as the world moved from the twentieth-century industrial paradigm into the twenty-first-century knowledge era. In the midst of organizational changes, Denning had been assigned to the "information" section of the company, and he began to see great potential for the World Bank in knowledge-sharing services. In searching for effective ways to communicate these radical ideas for change, Denning discovered the power of storytelling. His first success was with what he calls the Zambia story, which he began to deliver to groups of key organizational decision-makers. Here's the Zambia story as Denning shared it in *The Springboard:*

> Clearly the twenty-first century is going to be different. But how? The story of a health worker in Zambia offers the possibility of viewing the future, which, I suggest, is going to be like today.
>
> Thus, in June 1995, a health worker in Kamana, Zambia, logged on to the Center for Disease Control Web site and got the answer to a question on how to treat malaria.
>
> This true story happened, not in June 2015, but in June 1995. This is not a rich country: it is Zambia, one of the least developed countries in the world. It is not even the capital of the country: it is six hundred kilometers away. But the most striking aspect of the picture is this: our organization isn't in it. Our organization doesn't have its know-how and expertise organized in such a way that someone like the health worker in Zambia can have access to it. But just imagine if it had![11]

The Zambia story was not a quick fix for organizational change at the World Bank, but it put in motion what became an extremely effective overall communication strategy of organizational storytelling. You can sense from the sentence *"But the most striking aspect of the picture is this: our organization isn't in it"* how this story could indeed create a sense of urgency at the World Bank, as Kotter says is needed, and spark change, as Denning says is the desired response. Ultimately, the World Bank did adopt a radical new organization-wide strategy of knowledge sharing.

Crafting a Springboard Story

Denning advocates keeping the details of the springboard story nonspecific so that each listener can see possibilities according to his or her own perspective and imagination. Specifically referencing the "voice in the listener's head," Denning encourages the storyteller to embrace the potential partnership with that individual voice rather than fight to eliminate it. This is in keeping with the idea that successful change happens when a group of individuals owns an idea *as their own*. Ultimately, the power of the springboard story comes not from the story itself, but from the reaction it elicits in the listener.[12]

Other aspects of a successful springboard story are its brevity and its optimistic, visionary tone. By ending with phrases such as "what if we . . ." and "imagine if we were able to . . . ," the listener is invited to create his or her own ending, thus becoming an active partner in the emerging idea.

Stephen Denning lists a total of nine main elements of a good springboard story:[13]

- The change idea behind the story is crystal clear.
- The story is based on an actual example where the change was successfully implemented—that is, it's a true story.
- The story is told from the point of view of a single protagonist.
- The protagonist is typical of the audience.
- The story gives the date and place where it happened.
- The story makes clear what would have happened without the change idea.
- The story is told with little detail—it's told in minimalist fashion.
- The story has a positive tone—it has an authentically happy ending.
- The story is linked to the purpose to be achieved in telling it.

With these directions in mind, it's an interesting exercise to rewrite Drop Your Tools from a "change or die" cautionary tale to a more optimistic, inspirational story in the springboard form,

Drop Your Tools Rewritten
as Springboard Story for Libraries

Two groups of firefighters separated by four decades both faced a tragic end. What happened to them is similar to what we are facing, in that the very tools on which they depended and which helped them in the past had, at a point of critical need, become an encumbrance. The firefighters needed to drop their heavy firefighting tools so they could outrun the escalating fires. One man, the foreman Wagner Dodge of the 1949 Mann Gulch fire, was able to assess the situation and react quickly. In a flash of understanding, Dodge saw that his heavy firefighting tools, the ones he had always had success with in the past, were only hurting him in this changed environment. Dodge dropped his heavy tools. This gave him the extra speed he needed to escape danger, and he survived the fire. What if we could have that insight? What if we could identify which of our standard practices we could drop, and thus become truly nimble for the future?

The Drop Your Tools story rewritten as a springboard story has the requisite elements of connectedness, strangeness, and comprehension.[14] The springboard story should link the audience to a controlling idea and to a protagonist with whom the audience can relate. These days many librarians can relate to the image of being caught in a rapidly escalating fire, as they feel they are being overwhelmed by too much change too fast. It is easy to be drawn in to the story of the foreman who had a chance to escape; it is through this connection and resulting empathy that the listener's emotions begin to be engaged.

Denning also tells us that the springboard story must violate the listener's expectations in some way through surprise or a slight sense of incongruity. In our example, the surprise is that the firefighters are asked to drop their firefighting tools. However, Denning also says that the story must not be so strange that your listener begins to lose its potential as truth. Again, the listener must identify enough with the events as well as with the protagonist so that he can put himself into the story and maintain belief throughout its unfolding.

Finally, the story must be comprehensible. The story must be clear enough to generate understanding among the audience, without being so prescriptive that it shuts out imagination about what might happen if the lessons were enacted in their own organization.

The Drop Your Tools story has impact in its original form as well as in its springboard form. The exercise of rewriting a story for a new purpose leads to another useful skill: reframing a story to create a new meaning.

Story Reframing

It's important to think about the simple power of reframing a narrative, especially within a change project or a rapidly changing culture.[15] Or, if the story is just emerging, you can intentionally frame the narrative in a positive light to launch it most successfully. A situation can remain the same factually, but can be presented from a point of view of optimism or possibility. Remember the shoe salesmen mentioned in chapter 1 who looked at a shoeless population from two entirely different perspectives: *situation hopeless* versus *glorious opportunity.*[16]

Earlier in this chapter we looked at the Drop Your Tools story from two perspectives as well. In its first iteration, the focus was on the deaths of the firefighters; rewritten as a springboard story, the focus was on a survivor who might inspire us through his courageous behavior.

You should create intentional frames to your stories, being careful to maintain authenticity. Without authenticity, you put trust at risk. But without intentional framing, the story can veer off course. A leader at any level can reorient people by changing the dialogue. "People don't realize that they are responsible for those stories, and for making those stories live."[17] Framing the story of the library is a powerful tool for managing change and a powerful tool for managing organizational culture.

Thoughtful Transitions by Honoring the Past

Navigating change is not just about moving forward. It is about moving into the future within the context of the past and honoring the past as we leave it behind. Our life experiences stay with us and become a part of the overall fabric of our lives.

Previous parts of this chapter have focused on the emotional aspects of change, and one specific aspect of the Drop Your Tools story is the threat to people's identity created in that tool dropping. William Bridges emphasizes the importance of recognizing this critical aspect of loss in a person's process of coping with change.[18] Indeed, he compares the process to Elisabeth Kübler Ross's stages of grief, including denial, anger, and depression. Those who may resist change are trying to protect their world, and addressing this threat to their world is an essential element of change management. In thinking about change, a leader must identify what is being lost and by whom, and then mark the endings and treat them with respect. "Situational change hinges on the new thing, but psychological transition depends on letting go of the old reality and identity."[19] This letting-go process can generate significant feelings of loss.

Here's a memorable example of marking the end of an era for a library. In this story, the library director successfully guided the psychological transition from an old library building to a new one.

> There was a small liberal arts college where the library building was just terrible—one that could actually be classified with "sick building syndrome," where people suffered poor health effects from working there. Nothing was particularly good about the building; it was unattractive, uncomfortable, and nonfunctional. After much work over many years, the library raised enough money to build a new building adjacent to the old one. The library director gave the staff a great deal of ownership in the design and decoration of the new building, and people felt committed and enthusiastic as they watched the new construction. Finally, the building was finished, and the moving date approached. But suddenly it was evident that many people were having big problems with the move, and they started telling stories about how great the old building had been, and how they didn't want to move! They were struggling with the losses inherent in saying good-bye to the building and the identities they had built there.
>
> The library director decided they needed to commemorate their time in the old building, and honor its role in their past. She said, "Let's go on a farewell tour of the building." Everyone went—the whole staff. And the library director would say, "What happened that was funny or sad in this space? Can anybody remember?" And people told stories about every space in the whole building. The library director allowed them to live through history—the history of their time there—by sharing stories. And then together, they walked over to the new building.[20]

It's important to note that this story not only illustrates a meaningful farewell, but it also then becomes its own story—the story of how we said good-bye to an important part of our past. The farewell tour became a story in itself of saying good-bye to the old building and saying hello to the new building. Kathryn Deiss calls this "holding the past carefully in your hands" as you move forward. "If you don't allow people to carry what's treasured with them on this journey, they will not go."[21] This farewell story also could become a part of the library's sacred bundle, perhaps commemorated by a photo or a physical piece of the old building.

Doing a good job of honoring the past also means honoring the persons who are most interested in carrying it forward, persons Deiss calls *tradition bearers*. Giving the tradition bearer a place at the table, says Deiss, helps ensure that you stay steady and true to your mission in the midst of change. And this is another example where reorientation is useful; reframe *road blocker* stories as *tradition bearer* stories and include them in the overall conversation. Keeping the treasures of the past does not prevent you from moving forward; instead, it helps you move forward more thoughtfully, and thus with a much greater chance for ongoing success.

The next chapter looks at honoring the past and creating new futures within the broader context of the library service community. Once again, stories are a powerful tool in building and extending connections among libraries and those we serve.

Notes

1. The concept of the loss of the stable state comes from Donald Schon's 1971 book *Beyond the Stable State*. The metaphor of constant white water is a common one for today's rapidly evolving society.
2. John P. Kotter and Dan S. Cohen, *The Heart of Change* (Boston: Harvard Business School Press, 2002), 1.
3. John P. Kotter, "Introduction," in *The Heart of Change Field Guide,* by Dan. S. Cohen (Boston: Harvard Business School Press, 2005), xiv.
4. Kotter and Cohen, *Heart of Change,* 10–13.
5. Karl E. Weick, "Drop Your Tools: An Allegory for Organizational Studies," *Administrative Science Quarterly* 41 (July 1996): 301–13.
6. Ibid., 301, 304–5.
7. Karen Brown and Kate Marek, "Librarianship and Change: A Consideration of Weick's 'Drop Your Tools' Metaphor," *Library Administration and Management* 19, no. 2 (Spring 2005): 68–74.
8. Kotter and Cohen, *Heart of Change.*
9. John P. Kotter and Holger Rathgeber, *Our Iceberg Is Melting: Changing and Succeeding under Any Conditions* (New York: St. Martin's, 2005).
10. Stephen Denning, *The Springboard: How Storytelling Ignites Action in Knowledge-Era Organizations* (Boston: Butterworth-Heinemann, 2001), viii.
11. Ibid., 23–24.
12. Ibid., 129.
13. Stephen Denning, *The Leader's Guide to Storytelling* (San Francisco: Jossey-Bass, 2005), 51.
14. Denning, *Springboard,* 124–29.
15. This discussion grew from a conversation I had with my colleague Kathryn Deiss of the Association of College and Research Libraries.
16. Rosamund Zander and Benjamin Zander, *The Art of Possibility* (New York: Penguin, 2002), 9.

17. Kathryn Deiss, interviewed by Kate Marek, July 31, 2009.

18. William Bridges, *Managing Change: Making the Most of Transitions,* 2nd ed. (Cambridge, MA: De Capo, 2003).

19. Ibid., 7.

20. Kathryn Deiss, interviewed by Kate Marek, July 31, 2009.

21. Ibid.

chapter four
USING STORIES TO BUILD COMMUNITY

Stories are the glue that bind us together in communities . . .
and from this connectedness comes stories that heal.
—Lewis Mehl-Madrona, *Coyote Wisdom*

THERE ARE TWO ways to look at the assessment of library services. First, how good is the library? This includes our more traditional approach to assessment, where we count transactions, measure efficiency, and review costs. It is the second approach, however, that truly challenges us to be more thoughtful about library services, especially today in the midst of deep changes. We should also be asking, "How much good does the library do?" That question translates today to outcomes-based assessment and opens the door to rethinking our traditional bibliographic-centered programs and services. "How much good does the library do?" is a question that asks us to document the impacts of library services on our users and, more broadly speaking, on our communities.

This discussion of community is a timely topic; there is evidence that our personal, local engagement has weakened in recent decades. The issue of diminishing community connections in contemporary society was brought into the public conversation through Robert Putnam's "Bowling Alone" work.[1] Putnam argued that members of society are becoming more and more isolated from one another, finding community online and in niche issues rather than by gathering in public spaces. Even places such as bowling alleys were seeing shifts in how people used the space—more individual bowlers and a significant drop in bowling league activity. This growing isolation and self-interest has been further complicated by our society's increasing use of electronic interactions that give us the sense of connectedness but that do not replace true community.

What Is "Community"?

Writer and organizational consultant Peter Block published a book in 2008 called *Community: The Structure of Belonging*. It's that subtitle that, to me, eloquently conveys just exactly what we should focus on when talking about the concept of "community": the structure of what ties us together—in good ways—and gives us a sense of belonging to a larger group or purpose.

We face a real challenge in today's society to find a place of belonging. Life is fragmented and frantic, and despite our ubiquitous electronic connections, there is an absence of community connectedness. Despite our wired lifestyles, we still crave face-to-face social connections. Our human nature seeks belonging, but our Western individualistic culture often gets in the way of seeking bonds with others. Our society values personal independence and identity, but we are, in truth, essentially interdependent.

Robert Putnam studied governments in different regions of Italy in the first stages of his work. Though the governments he studied seemed very similar, they had very different levels of effectiveness; through further investigation he discovered that it was long-standing traditions of overall civic engagement that made a positive difference. It was the degree of *social capital* that was important, a term Putnam defines as "features of social organization such as networks, norms, and social trust that facilitate coordination and cooperation for mutual benefit."[2] Or, as Peter Block explains, the well-being of a community is defined by the quality of its members' relationships with one another and their sense of trust in each other. "We need to create a community where each citizen has the experience of being connected to those around them and knows that their safety and success are dependent on the success of all others."[3] Healthy communities, and thus a healthy society, transform isolation into a sense of caring for the whole.

It's important to note that the degree of social capital is not dependent on uniformity or conformity in a community. Indeed, diversity is an important element of a healthy group. When a group is composed of one mind, it tends to be inward looking, and community disintegrates into divisions of smaller networks. The healthier group is composed of different types of people and *bridges* the divisions. Implicit in this healthy group of diverse people, though, is a sense of shared purpose and common understanding. This is where shared narrative can be a useful tool, helping people gain knowledge of strangers that leads to shared trust.

How can libraries be involved in creating structures of belonging in order to enhance community? One way is simply to recognize the value of community and build this into the mission of the organization. An emphasis on this aspect of service will then be reflected in everything from our libraries' programming to their physical spaces. (See, for example, the libraries profiled in chapter 5.) Other types of activities focus more specifically on inviting that shared narrative. Two excellent examples will be explored later in this chapter. First, it is helpful to look more closely at some consistent themes in Peter Block's book that offer us an exciting template for libraries' potential in the area of creating community.

Creating a New Direction

Despite our connective technologies and our global economic relations, Block says we are living in an age of isolationism. There is a pronounced "absence of belonging" in our lives. "Our isolation occurs because western culture, our individualistic narrative, the inward attention of our institutions and our professions, and the messages from our media all fragment us. We are broken into pieces."[4] (For example, due to media spin, the fear of crime went up in the 1990s and early 2000s, despite the fact that the crime rate actually dropped in America.)[5]

Building healthy communities gives us a way to combat that and to accomplish *collective transformation*. Building social capital, or *social fabric,* as Block calls it, is accomplished in small but important ways in collaboration with others. A strong message from Block is to concentrate on people's gifts rather than deficiencies and to further reframe our worlds by reframing our stories. Our relationship with the past will always define our future, but we must use stories to move forward rather than having those stories define us in unexamined ways. I looked a little more closely at using stories to say good-bye to the past in chapter 3, but the issue is relevant here as well. Similar in concept to prototypical feuding families such as the Montagues and Capulets or the Hatfields and McCoys, old stories that are left unresolved continue to haunt us and create cycles of tragedy. Instead, Block encourages us to ask: "What can we create together?"

This opportunity to work together to create a shared future is dependent on changing the structures through which we engage one another. Sharing each other's stories is one critical way to learn more about each other, share in others' life experiences, and truly begin to care for each other. With mutual caring comes restoration, mutual accountability, and true social fabric. Block emphasizes that with the intentional, deliberate, and proactive use of a communal story, built on diverse individual histories, people can set a positive future agenda and truly begin to create community. Block calls this process of creating a communal story the creation of "the future that we choose to live into."

An Opportunity for Libraries

Block's book is a powerful examination of our local community services and their potential to improve lives based on establishing, renewing, and strengthening connections among citizens. His work is a template for looking at the potential of libraries to expand their role in a changing society. Block challenges communities to ask: How do we choose to be together, and what do we choose to create together? And, for us, how could the library participate in that conversation?

Reflecting on this concept, it seems that libraries do indeed have exciting potential to participate in collective transformation. One key Block emphasizes is the power of small but important opportunities of being together to create a sense of belonging; he also encourages us to focus on individuals' gifts rather than their deficiencies. Libraries, no matter what type, regularly create opportunities for community members to be together, and we do build on gifts rather than deficiencies. We can concentrate, then, on intentionally building these efforts into our missions and on creating programs and services designed to fulfill that mission emphasis.

Librarians place an extremely high value on service to users, so much so that we often speak of service as a core professional value. In recent years, our perspective has shifted in a subtle but key way in that we are focusing on creating those services from the user's point of view, as opposed to our own assumptions of what that service should be. We can improve library service by understanding our service community better, and we can also improve the community itself by helping to strengthen bonds among its members.

One of the things storytelling does best is to bring people together. Whether it is a personal story shared among library staff, a story relating the library's impact on a community member, or a story shared between community members themselves such as the following examples in this chapter, talking to one another carries great dividends.

Two Examples

Two projects, Agora: Storyboard of Your Life and the Living Library, provide an excellent point of reference for discussing the library's transformational potential in building the social fabric of our communities.

Agora: Storyboard of Your Life

In the fall of 2007, three men from the public library in Delft, Netherlands, set out on a bus tour across the United States. Their goal was to visit libraries from New York to California, stopping to collect library stories and best practices. The group referred to themselves as "Shanachies," a term they took from Ireland's old-fashioned storyteller; the cross-country trek was dubbed the Shanachie Tour.[6] The Shanachie motto was Keep Stories, Make Stories, Share Stories. The three men, Jaap van de Geer, Erik Boekesteijn, and Geert van den Boogaard, interviewed librarians and library users and posted web videos along the way. Their final destination was the Internet Librarian Conference, where they showed their videos and told the stories they had found.

The Shanachies' home library is called the DOK Library Concept Center,[7] where the mission is to become the world's most modern library.[8] One of the ways they are working toward that mission is to expand the library's potential with regard to this traditional activity of collecting and sharing stories—aided by creative applications of the newest technologies. One result is the DOK Agora: Storyboard of Your Life program. This local program has exciting potential for all libraries to provide a platform for community members to share their stories.

> One of the biggest projects we're working on is DOK Agora, "the storyboard of your life." On huge screens in the library, it is possible to present an exhibition of whatever you, as a patron, think is important and of value to the community. Imagine that your grandmother is about to celebrate her 85th birthday. Wouldn't it be great to make an exhibition of her life and show it in the library? A camera crew will interview relatives and friends. They will go to the places where she lived and worked. The final presentation will contain the music and art she loves in a cross-media tribute to a person, a time, and a city. People in the library will see this, recognize things, talk about their own memories, and share their stories. It is a great way of promoting social cohesion.[9]

You can also participate in the DOK Agora project by going to the library and finding cultural heritage materials there and from other local historical collections. Through partnerships with other local organizations, extensive local collections of maps, documents, and images have been digitized and made available to the public. One way the public has access to these and other community records is through a Microsoft Surface table, a computer that looks like a large coffee table with a glass top.[10] The MS Surface interacts directly with digital devices such as cameras and cell phones and is operated through a giant touch screen rather than by a mouse or a keyboard. Several people can work together at the Surface table, easily enabling collaborative experiences.[11]

You get started at the Surface table by scanning your library card bar code just as you would at the self-checkout station or at the grocery store. The table reads your bar code and brings up some options. One option is to connect to your current address (retrieved from your patron record) and display a variety of local cultural heritage materials from the database. From this starting point, community members can find, share, and make all sorts of stories.

To connect this project to the broader community, every three months the DOK highlights a new theme, such as stories from a local business or stories from one particular neighborhood. At the end of three months of collecting and sharing stories on an individual basis, the library hosts a community-wide event where people come together to present their stories in public and listen to others. This final element of the project creates an additional link in the creation of the communal story, as people hear new stories that connect to their own and learn more about their community and their neighbors.

Here's how something like this might work for me. My mother grew up in Dallas, Texas, in the 1930s and 1940s. She often talked of her grandmother's house on Ross Avenue, where she spent a lot of time in her youth. But my mother died over twenty-five years ago, and thus identifying family heritage material has always been difficult. If the Dallas Public Library offered its own version of the Agora project, I could perhaps find an image of my great-grandmother's house, which was torn down before I was born to make room for a new apartment complex. Because Ross Avenue was a major boulevard in that period of Dallas history, there is a good chance I could find something among all the collected early Dallas photos. If I were able to find the house and, through the database, connect it to my great-grandparents' names, I could link in my own memory to stories my mother told me of the house and the time she spent there. I could add my stories to the database, and other people could find those stories and connect them to their own. I might, for example, be able to find some distant relatives, or some Dallas residents whose family members might have worked for my great-grandmother when she ran a small boardinghouse at that address.

Finally, if I had worked on my project during a period when the library was highlighting Dallas neighborhoods of the 1930s and 1940s, I could participate in the community-wide event and share my story with a wider public audience. By building these memories together, in the presence of others, as Block would say, my personal experience is enhanced and the collective community memory is also enhanced.

There is transformative power in building connections through shared stories; the library is the perfect organization to facilitate such sharing. In doing so, the library expands its role from a community information resource to a key player in transforming community. Let me introduce another project to you that demonstrates libraries' opportunities to build community.

Living Library Project

In a Living Library event, volunteers from the community come together to share their unique stories in face-to-face meetings at the library. Those who are sharing stories are called *Books,* and the listeners are called *Readers.* The idea originated not far from the DOK, and it is another wonderful example of building community through structured story sharing. Ronni Abergel is the Danish organizer who launched the first Living Library in 2000; his goal was to increase tolerance and understanding among people with diverse backgrounds and interests. Since then public libraries, academic libraries, and community centers in over forty countries have organized Living Library events.

At the event, Living Books are checked out by Readers, and together they have a conversation lasting about thirty minutes. A Reader may then choose to check out another Living Book, leaving the original Living Book available for checkout by another Reader. In this report from a Living Library project in east London, the Living Books included a Rwandan refugee, a policeman, a witch, and a stay-at-home dad.[12]

> At one table, a Rwandan refugee explains to a listener why immigrants cannot be dismissed both as a drain on the public purse and a threat to local jobs. At another, a transgender individual relates why she felt biologically compelled to change sex. An Indian atheist and a Muslim are setting forth their worldview to "readers."
>
> And those "books" that aren't currently checked out—among them a witch, a funeral director, a medium, and a police officer—are swapping stories in the back room, eating sandwiches, and waiting for their next appointment.
>
> All of the "books" are unpaid volunteers, as are the organizers, recruited for the event.[13]

The Living Library concept is quickly gaining popularity across the world, with its most rapid expansion here in the United States. The project's website at http://living-library.org keeps an up-to-date list of Living Library activity as well as many resources for planning events.[14] One of the earliest events in this country was at the Santa Monica Public Library in October 2008. The event was described in *Library Journal:*

One visitor, a Southern California librarian, wrote on her blog about meeting with a homeless advocate, who advised her that giving food coupons to homeless people is better than money and [explained] why Santa Monica has such a large homeless population. The advocate ultimately imparted a moving story about how she had become homeless herself and, after she got back on her feet, dedicated herself to advocacy work. "What started off as just a curiosity—so what happens at the Living Library, anyway?—ended up being a profound experience," wrote the librarian.[15]

And from the librarian herself, from her subsequent blog post:

The place was abuzz when my husband and I arrived. Library patrons were jockeying for a chance to speak with an available Book, while volunteers, wearing gray "Don't Judge a Book by Its Cover" t-shirts, directed participants to conference rooms and tables. I signed up to meet with Rachel, the homeless advocate, at 2:30 PM. As I waited my turn, I reviewed a list of suggested questions to ask my Living Book:

Why did you want to tell your story? What makes you stereotypical/not stereotypical? How have you been accepted/not accepted in society? What is the most rewarding experience you have had? What is your biggest obstacle? Do you have a defining moment? What was it?

I chose instead to ask whether or not I should give money to street people (the answer: no—it is much better to give food coupons or actual food) and why Santa Monica has such a large homeless population. I also asked what services are available for local homeless folks.

What I learned: (1) many of the people living on the streets of Santa Monica actually grew up in the area before becoming, for whatever reason, homeless; (2) according to the only two census counts conducted locally (in 2005 and 2007), the number of homeless people is dropping, possibly because of the good work being done by social service agencies countywide; and (3) although no one likes living on the street, it can be difficult to motivate people to change their situation even if that change is for the better—loss of dignity is one of the most powerful barriers keeping homeless people from improving their lives.

The most surprising moment came, however, when I asked Rachel how she had become an advocate for the homeless.

"Do you have a degree in sociology?" I wondered aloud.

She smiled and said that she had started off in banking many years ago, but then, after suffering a bout of severe depression, had become homeless herself. Supported and cared for by several agencies, she decided to dedicate her life to helping other homeless people once she got back on her feet. We then spent the rest of the all-too-short session talking about how rewarding her work is. At the end of 30 minutes, I shook Rachel's hand and thanked her for sharing her story with me.

What started off as just a curiosity—so what happens at the Living Library, anyway?—ended up being a profound experience where I not only learned more about homelessness, but also met someone who overcame seemingly insurmountable odds to now help others better themselves.

I hope more libraries will consider tapping into the rich depths of their local communities to share the unique knowledge of their own Living Books.[16]

The rich experiences facilitated through these two projects—the Agora project and the Living Library project—could easily be organized at any kind of library, celebrating communities of any definition. The discussion of community relationships is relevant to all types of libraries, because *community* for a library is not necessarily defined by geography. For a public library, the primary service population is geographic, but other types of libraries' service populations are defined by those libraries' individual institutional missions. Academic libraries, for example, define their primary community as the institution's students, faculty, staff, and alumni. Special libraries' service population, and thus community, are specific to their own institutional mission and purpose. School libraries have a community focused on the more specific populations of students and parents. Whatever type of library, there is truly great potential to strengthen community by structuring opportunities for story sharing.

The strength in the library (whatever the type) is how well it serves its local community. In thinking about a strategic plan or a broad strategy for the future, the needs of your own community should be at the very heart of your discussion. But successful service is about more than just the direct needs of the community (such as more languages represented in the collection or longer hours of operation). It's also very much about being a key player in *building community*—strengthening the ties that bind your residents and patrons. "Communal transformation . . . occurs when people get connected to those who were previously strangers."[17] When we strengthen connections through building and sharing stories, we participate in strengthening the vital social fabric of our communities.

Notes

1. "Bowling Alone," Robert Putnam's research article on the loss of community connections, was published in 1995. He expanded his work into a book, *Bowling Alone: The Collapse and Revival of American Community* (New York: Simon and Schuster, 2000).
2. Robert Putnam, "Bowling Alone: America's Declining Social Capital," *Journal of Democracy* 6, no. 1 (1995): 67.
3. Peter Block, *Community: The Structure of Belonging* (San Francisco: BK, 2008), 5.
4. Ibid., 2.
5. Ibid., 56.
6. Find out more about the Shanachie Tour 2007 at www.shanachietour.com.
7. The initials "DOK" come from the library's emphasis on three main collections: Music and Film ("Discotake" in Dutch), Literature ("Openbare Bibliotheek"), and Art ("Kunstcentrum"). See Erik Boekesteijn, "Discover Innovations at DOK, Holland's 'Library Concept Center,'" *Marketing Library Services* 22, no. 2 (March/April 2008), available online at www.infotoday.com/MLS/mar08/Boekesteijn.shtml.
8. See the English-language version of the DOK website, www.dok.info/.
9. Boekesteijn, "Discover Innovations at DOK."
10. See www.microsoft.com/surface/Pages/Product/WhatIs.aspx for a more complete explanation of this technology.
11. Ibid.
12. Mark Rice-Oxley, "Borrow a Muslim? A 'Living Library' to Prick Stereotypes," *Christian Science Monitor,* June 4, 2008.
13. Ibid.
14. Another excellent resource for organizing Living Library projects is available through the WebJunction webinar, "Living Library Projects," July 22, 2009. See www.webjunction.org.
15. Norman Oder, "'Living Library' Débuts in Santa Monica," *Library Journal* 133, no. 19 (November 15, 2008): 15. The blog referenced in this quote from *Library Journal* is a wonderfully reflective essay about one librarian's experience visiting a Living Library event. It can be found at La Vida Biblioteca, "Living Library," http://lavidabiblioteca .blogspot.com/2008/10/living-library.html.
16. La Vida Biblioteca, "Living Library."
17. Block, *Community,* 60.

chapter five
TELLING STORIES THROUGH BUILDINGS

Architecture is not based on concrete and steel, and elements of the soil. It is based on wonder. It is a story that is told through its hard materials.
—Daniel Libeskind

Architecture as Story

Architects are keenly aware of the messages they send, or the stories they tell, through the design and construction of physical spaces. Daniel Libeskind, master plan architect for the reconstruction of the World Trade Center site, refers to architecture as "a language"[1] and uses seventeen words to describe his own design philosophies.[2] Chief among those words is "communicative," which he specifically contrasts with "mute." To Libeskind, architecture tells a story based on wonder, told through hard materials that express "a struggle against impossibilities," such as through the pyramids, temples, cathedrals, and our great cities. And to Libeskind the story told through architecture is ongoing, continually evolving through our own use and enjoyment of the physical spaces we create.[3]

It's not hard to understand the visual symbolism in architecture, and our great traditional library buildings stand as excellent examples of "temples of knowledge." In addition, more is being written about the social use of spaces. Social spaces can also be structured symbolically, inviting narrative through their visual presentation and through their use. Sociologists examine this concept and assess the communication between space and people, and librarians can make use of this research as well.[4] The physical design of a space, its arrangement, decoration, and furnishings all play a role in our emotional response to that environment.

Library buildings have an added story element. Jeffrey Scherer, an architect who has worked with librarians and libraries for over thirty years, and who was a principal team member on the St. Paul Central Library project, says people tend to think of their own stories when they go into a library. "They tend to carry with them a complex mix of emotional and childhood and familial memories of what the library meant to them, and why it's important, as well as an aspirational side, which is what the library will unlock in their future story."[5]

This is not to indicate that the library building should tell a generic story, however. Each community is unique, and the library building should convey the language and the culture of its own people, their history, and their future.

Stories Told through Four Libraries

Picture the beginnings of our country and the communities that sprang up in the time of colonial America, with prototypical New England mills and ubiquitous stone fences, full of colonial charm. Now shift your thinking westward; consider the romance of Lake Michigan and the powerful Chicago lakefront. Next on your mind's-eye journey west, visualize the old-world beauty of St. Paul, Minnesota, with its classically designed, historic downtown buildings such as the famous St. Paul Cathedral atop the city's highest downtown hill. Finally, end your westward scan in sunny Southern California, the home of Disneyland with the pervasive influence of Walt Disney himself.

Each of these communities has a story to tell, and the businesses and services that exist in these areas are reflective of those broader stories. Such is the case with four libraries (starting from where we left off in the west, then heading back toward the east): Cerritos Public Library in Cerritos, California; St. Paul Public Central Library; Loyola University Chicago Information Commons; and the public library in Darien, Connecticut. These libraries have all completed major renovations, expansions, or new construction projects within the past decade; their new public spaces consciously and eloquently tell the stories of their individual communities as well as tales of their own local information services.

In gathering information about the renovation and expansion projects of these libraries, three strong commonalities were evident: emphasis on the library as a "third place" within the community, designing from the user's point of view, and designing as a twenty-first-century library space.

The Concept of the "Third Place"

The "third place" concept was introduced by sociologist Ray Oldenburg in his 1989 book *The Great Good Place*. Oldenburg describes the third place as separate from our first place of home and from our second life-place of work. An additional, third space is a public gathering place outside of both home and work where people can interact and enjoy life. Examples of third places from Oldenburg's work include post offices, cafés, and local bars.

Libraries were not on Oldenburg's original list of great good places (his other term for the third place), but our profession has enthusiastically embraced the concept of the third place as being very much a part of our mission. Looking at Oldenburg's list of third place characteristics, you can see why.[6] Oldenburg's third place is open, free, inclusive, and local. A third place is neutral ground—there is no political or institutional agenda associated with the space. *Conversation* is one of the most important aspects of third place gatherings, and the highly inclusive nature of the third place helps to unify the neighborhood, mix the generations, and provide for a rich interactive exchange. Good third places are places for fun as well as for intellectual and political discourse.

The concept of the third place has become quite dominant in librarians' professional dialogue. As we continue to move toward the redefinition of the physical library through our evolution from print to digital resources, we have consciously examined the concept of "library as place." The reduction in floor space committed to print material has opened up new possibilities in terms of programs and services, as well as a focused attention on the way people prefer to *use* library spaces. Today we look at the many different ways the physical library in America can carry forward our unique mission in terms of education, literacy, information access, and cultural stewardship.

Designing from the User's Point of View

All the library planners in this chapter specifically described their emphasis on designing from the user's point of view. This shift away from designing spaces based on librarians' workflow and on the physical artifact of the book to a very conscious focus on the user was a priority in each case. This new perspective resulted in a wide range of choices, from the language used in naming specific library spaces to the choice of themes for certain areas.

Listening to users in the design process emerged as a key part of the planning stage. For example, Jeffrey Scherer from St. Paul, Minnesota, conducts numerous community focus group meetings for his library building projects. (He conducted thirty-six for his firm's Fayetteville, Arkansas, project, for example.) Something as subtle as the strategic placement of a literacy center can be an important part of the design; administrators may want to stress the library's emphasis on literacy education by including a prominent literacy training room front and center, but sensitivity to the users of that space makes its placement in a more secluded part of the building more appropriate. Listening to the users in the planning stages helps planners understand the power of these individual story threads.[7]

Creating the Twenty-First-Century Library

All of the libraries included in this chapter were planning and designing their building projects within a few years of the turn of the century. The planners of the new library in Darien, Connecticut, articulated the importance of this new century mark most clearly, saying they wanted to build the first of the new libraries, not the last of the old. Rapid technological changes in the last few decades have made it clear that we are in a new era of information services, and all of these library planners were keenly focused on making their buildings effective for this new era.

These common elements—the creation of a "third place" for the community, creating services and spaces from the user's point of view, and designing for the twenty-first-century library—came together in unique ways for each of the four communities. A strong partnership between the libraries and their architects also proved to be essential, and although this may seem to be evident as a requirement for success, the conversations I had with the library planners helped me to understand that their highly effective library-architect partnerships created an active synergy of thought, where everyone who was involved learned as they went along and participated actively in the evolution of the library's story and design.[8]

The four libraries in this chapter created and now maintain new spaces that are very physically different from one another, each being directly reflective of their individual community's ongoing local story. All of them are exciting and beautiful and provide public spaces that are not only great good places for society, but are great good places *to be* as individuals and for communities.

Cerritos Public Library

The most overt and fully articulated use of story in the planning and design of a new library is found in Cerritos, California, where a new library building was dedicated in March 2002.[9] Waynn Pearson, the former library director who led the process, highlights the use of story lines as an essential communication tool for both architecture and design. "A compelling story line provides a planning framework yet lets your imagination soar."[10] When Pearson speaks of his inspiration, three key areas emerge: Walt Disney's theme parks, the concept of a strong user experience as described by Joseph Pine and James Gilmore in their book *The Experience Economy,* and the design and concepts of Frank Gehry's Guggenheim Museum Bilbao.

Conceiving of something completely different is no easy task when thinking about libraries. Our libraries' well-known and much-loved legacy story as a human, and then American, institution provides us with strength, but also limits us to what we already know. Breaking out of our conceptual box takes great imagination—which, actually, is in no short supply in Southern California. Indeed, human imagination and creativity have become a celebrated part of the Southern California/Hollywood culture. Imagination is so highly valued at the Disney Corporation that there is a specific vocation as a "Disney Imaginer." Indeed, Waynn Pearson led a planning process in Cerritos that was more accurately described as "imagineering" than planning; this subtle reframing helped all the planners to move out of the "library" box and to stay there.

The most compelling element of the Cerritos Public Library project from the point of view of story is its foundational emphasis on theming, and in particular as based on the ideas of Walt Disney and the work of his longtime associate John Hench. Walt Disney's idea for Disneyland was to create a place where "adults and children could experience together some of the wonders of life and adventure, and feel better because of it."[11] He was inspired to this by his own dissatisfaction with existing amusement parks as he experienced them with his young daughters.[12] It is fitting, then, to think of the library as a beneficiary of this thinking: a library should also be a place where people of all generations can come—together or separately—to enjoy the riches of human culture.

Beyond theming and story lines, the Cerritos Public Library brainstorming focused on imagining the "learner's experience." "You've got to talk about the library experience before you do anything else. The building will come about because of what you develop in terms of the library experience."[13] Pearson envisioned a library that could offer a multi-sensory learning experience as the library's key product and looked to entertainment and commerce for ideas.

Themes in the Cerritos Public Library

With "the experience library" as an overall framework for the new library's core stories, the library planners created numerous unique spaces designed to offer a variety of services and learning experiences. The current library director, Don Buckley, eloquently describes the library in terms of the underlying story concepts and the individual pieces of that story:

> When former City Librarian Waynn Pearson talks about the Experience Library project he often says that they weren't building a library, they were telling a story. There are two main story lines in the library. The first is "Honoring the past, imagining the future," which relates best to the exterior of the building and most of the inside. The Children's Library has its own theme, "Save the Planet, Earth's Delicate Balance."
>
> Standing outside looking from the Tsunami fountain toward the library, you can see the curvilinear titanium exterior rising up over the much more traditional rectilinear white sides of the 1987 expansion. The past (albeit recent) and future come together dramatically from this angle.

As you walk through the front door and move to the right (a natural way-finding tendency), you enter the Old World section, which is filled with leather-bound and fine press editions. The area represents what most people think of as a classic library with lots of dark wood and chandeliers. This is the first stop on our journey through architectural time.

Further down Main Street and again on the right lies the Craftsman area. Along the way you will see museum exhibits integrated in the library itself. Craftsman style was very popular in southern California in the early twentieth century. Our area features Stickley furniture with many different types of seating, including traditional chairs at a long study table, easy chairs, rocking chairs, couches, and Prairie chairs. There is a grandfather clock as well. The computers here are housed in a wood structure constructed in the Craftsman style. There is a large plein air painting on the wall, replicating a popular style of the period.

Directly across from the Craftsman area is the Young Adult area based on Art Deco/Streamline Moderne style. This motif was chosen by local teens. The entryway is based on the Pan-Pacific Auditorium and leads to an area dominated by shades of pink and purple. Many visitors have commented that they recognized this as the Young Adult area based on the ambience and décor alone, a significant way-finding advantage.

Ascending the stairs, you reach the World Traditions area, home to our very substantial Asian-language collection. The décor here is a mélange of Art Deco with Asian influences that we call Shanghai Deco. Once again, the style is tied to the content of the area. Ascending still further on a diagonal brings you to the 21st Century level representing the library of the future. There is no wood used in the public areas on this level. Light comes from every angle; the stack ends glow, and light bounces off stack top reflectors or a bright metal ceiling. The reference desk represents a time machine and is identified by a fiber-optically projected sign. There are over ninety public-access computers on this level.

The Children's area with its Save the Planet theme is a wonderland for children of all ages. From the portal of giant books, to the green screen where kids can put themselves in the picture or film clips, to the forty-foot-long T-Rex named Stan, this is an area that attracts people time after time. This is an environment that is both interactive and multi-sensory. You can touch the foot of the dinosaur, or see its history at the touch of a button. You can hear the sounds of the rain forest as you embrace

the banyan tree that stands at the far end of the room. There is a Little
Theatre for storytimes and an Art Studio for crafts and homework help.
The pièce de résistance is the Aquarium, which holds 15,000 gallons of
saltwater. It is home to numerous species of fish and two different kinds
of shark. The earth and its history are well represented in the Children's
Library.[14]

These physical spaces with individual themes were essential in creating
the multi-sensory learning experience that Pearson envisioned. But he also
emphasizes that the library was not creating experiences for the sake of experiences: "It's about creating a spark . . . something that triggers the guest's
or user's imagination in terms of learning."[15] The stories told through the
Cerritos Public Library's beautiful building help to do just that.

St. Paul Public Central Library

Moving east, our next stop is the powerful historic building of the Central
Library in downtown St. Paul, Minnesota. Although Cerritos designed a new
public library building based on rapid community growth and change, in
the late 1990s St. Paul's public library planners were in the midst of a new
community focus on preserving the historic architecture of the city's center. Debbie Willms, administration services manager of the St. Paul Public
Central Library, speaks of the Central Library building as a real asset to the
city. "There never would have been any question about tearing down the
building."[16] The Central Library is a key part of the city's downtown area,
and that, in turn, is a very important aspect of the library's own story. "It has
always been a very important part of how we think about ourselves—that we
have this architectural entity in downtown St. Paul."[17]

The "Central Library History" section of the library's website gives us
basic information about the building and its architecture. I include it here to
give you a sense of the beauty of the building and also because the text eloquently conveys the value of the building to its community:

> [The] Central Library is Italian Renaissance revival in style. Some features
> marking the style include the round arched windows, the Palladian style
> entrances, the large stonework, the balustrade surrounding the building,

the rondel features near the arched windows, use of classical columns and pilasters, and the cornice capping the structure. The style was continued throughout the interior of the Library.

The exterior of the Library is of Tennessee marble, while the interior is finished in gray Mankato stone. Blue Rutland and golden vein Formosa marble are also used in select areas.

The original wood work in the building is a gray stained maple. The floors of the three main rooms were originally of compressed cork and have been recreated in the recent renewal project.

The Kellogg Boulevard courtyard, including a new entrance, was also redesigned during the renovations.

—Central Library History (constructed 1914–1917, opened in 1917)[18]

For some years leading up to the renovation project, however, attempts to accommodate changing technologies had taken a significant toll on the building. Wiring and conduit were stretched everywhere, beautiful painted ceilings had been covered up, and unattractive lighting fixtures had been put in place.

Two key story lines for the renovation project emerged: first, returning the library to its original glory and, second, making the space more usable as a public space for the twenty-first century. Both of these stories were essential messages to the citizens of St. Paul, where the historical context was valued, but where vibrant community library services are also highly prized and heavily used. Willms notes that popular building tours focus on the site as a historical treasure. At the same time, however, the library has an active story line emphasizing the library beyond the building as a community resource and a virtual realm.

The planners' ability to accomplish both the restoration and the modernization was due in large part to their collaboration with the St. Paul architectural firm of Meyer, Scherer and Rockcastle, and in particular the principal team member, Jeffrey Scherer. Scherer has a strong professional focus on building renovation for new uses. He works extensively with both libraries and with historical restorations, and he makes powerful use of the legacy story in his work. According to Scherer, there was a very specific narrative threaded through the St. Paul Public Central Library building when it was originally designed; that narrative included the importance of St. Paul in the early twentieth century as the state's industrial and governmental hub and the contemporary perception of how libraries should look based on their role as containers of the world's knowledge. The challenge was to respect that foundational story, but introduce the new narrative of the twenty-first century.

To accomplish this, they made radical changes in the building's interior that included tearing out seven stories of closed stacks to make four public floors and inserting modern, transitional thresholds that signal to people as they go from one historical artifact to another that there has been intervention.[19] This "was in itself declaring that the stacks were figuratively and literally open to the public, and that the floors would be contiguous, and that that space would be given over not only to collection but also for readers."[20]

The renovation and modernization of the Public Central Library is genuinely reflective of the ongoing story of the St. Paul community, where heritage, literacy, education, and community are all highly valued. Scherer and his coauthor Sam Demas call this matching of community to place "place-making" to achieve an *esprit de place,* or spirit of place. "The successful library building, with its programs and its staff, creates a sense of connection to the values, traditions, and intellectual life of the community, and helps the patron participate in building its future."[21]

Loyola University Chicago Information Commons

Collaboration, connectivity, and community: these three words formed the beginning of a story told on Chicago's Lake Michigan lakefront for the Loyola University community. There, a new library expansion and construction project began to take shape in the first years of the twenty-first century. Collaboration, connectivity, and community came to be known as the "three Cs," and their use formed a conceptual base for the library's new architecture, engineering, design, and decoration. Each of the words played its own unique role in the design of the new Information Commons, which opened in April 2009.

Robert Seal, dean of libraries at Loyola, moved to Chicago in 2005 to help build the library's expansion and new construction. He recalls a point soon after he joined the planning process when he was due to pitch the information commons concept to key decision-makers for the new library construction. Reflective of Stephen Denning's emphasis on the brevity of a good springboard story, Seal remembers thinking about his upcoming presentation to the university trustees. "I knew they didn't have a lot of time for a lot of detail, so what I wanted to do was stress some concepts that we were thinking about, that we were going to build the project on. So we came up with the idea of what I call the three Cs, the first being collaboration, the second being connectivity, and the third being community."[22]

In our conversation, Seal proceeded to describe the three Cs in more detail:

> A lot of projects these days in class are collaborative in nature—a lot of team learning going on, and in fact the students just like to study together anyway, as they always have. . . .
>
> The connectivity part was pretty obvious; this is a high-tech building, in the Internet age, and students are connected all the time to their family and friends, and to professors. . . .
>
> We really wanted a place for our students to be attracted to, based on the sociologists' concept of the "third place," a place that's not work or home, but a place you like to be when you're not at one of those two places. It could be the café down at the corner, it could be a clubhouse, it could be your church. It could be any number of places. But we wanted the Information Commons to be that third place, and have a community sort of a feel to it so that students would feel welcome and they would want to come to the building.
>
> And along with those three Cs, we knew that we wanted a flexible building for the future, so that in the future we could make changes, as certainly changes will come. We wanted the building therefore to be very open—architecturally open, so that we could make changes. And also, I think the president wanted to be able to look through the building and see Lake Michigan. So that was a real factor there.[23]

The story of the three Cs became Bob Seal's springboard story for Loyola's new library building, or the new Information Commons, as he began to call it. This story is still in use, as a legacy story for the origins of the building, as a living story to describe the building to visitors, and as a new springboard story for further library renovation and expansion planned on the Loyola campus.[24]

The original story enabled the planners to focus on physical and social spaces that carried out the plan: a visually stunning new building framed with floor-to-ceiling windows on each of its four floors. The building in-cludes hundreds of networked desktop and laptop computers, ubiquitous wireless connectivity, web portals to electronic resources, and a wide va-riety of social spaces with comfortable seating. There is an adjacent café and an open, flexible design that allows for future reconfiguration as needs arise.

There was also a deliberate attempt to offset the potential coldness of so much technology, as well as the often icy mood of Lake Michigan in the winter. To accomplish this, the planners chose warm furnishings and appoint-ments. Seal recalls:

> We could have made it have kind of an industrial feel, with lots of metal, and chairs on wheels, and funny-shaped tables and so on, and a lot of places have done that very successfully. [But] we were greatly influenced by the need to make the building feel warmer, because being right on the lake, especially in the wintertime, the kind of building I just described . . . could have a very cold feel to it. I think the idea was that having wood furniture, which is very traditional, and nice carpeting, and some wood paneling [as suggested] by the president, really changed it a lot. So that did have an influence on the design, very definitely. You kind of feel like you are in a traditional library in a way, and yet the tools you have are very different.[25]

Seal truly believes that Loyola's Information Commons has become the indoor gathering place for the campus, with a new adjacent green space as its outdoor center. He, along with the other librarians I interviewed, em-phasized the importance of responding to users' needs. "In the past we just kind of assumed we knew what users needed, so we made our rules and built our buildings, and didn't ask for much user feedback. Now we're just the opposite."[26]

The three Cs continue to be the central story of Loyola's Information Commons, and it has become a community story rather than a planner's story. The students and faculty tell the story of the three Cs to visitors as they show off the space and explain its design, and the three Cs are used to describe the building to the public via the library's website.[27] But this build-ing in all its beauty is not the story itself; rather, it tells a tale of a university library focused on its users' needs for a collaborative space for gathering and study, a space that enables ubiquitous connections and one that ambitiously fosters community.

Darien Library, Connecticut

Many other libraries are also stepping up to the challenges of the twenty-first century with dramatic changes in buildings that reflect new service models. Our tour ends back on the East Coast, where the Darien, Connecticut, library planners emphasized both technology and New England tradition in the town's recently completed new building, which debuted in January 2009.[28] When Director Louise Parker Berry and the planning team were contemplating the new public library building, she knew she did not want to build just another lovely library. "About four or five years ago, we had a clear idea that we didn't want to build the last of the old libraries—we wanted to build the first of the new libraries."[29] In addition to an emphasis on technology and twenty-first-century usage, however, the Darien planners wanted a timeless building that offered the community the sense of a permanent and important local library presence. The new building accomplishes all that. It is in the center of the town, and the strong stone building manages to convey both permanence and flexibility.

The building includes a strong green energy component and was the first building in New England to gain LEED (Leadership in Energy and Environmental Design) green building certification. This deliberate combination of Old World New England charm and a cutting-edge emphasis on sustainability and technology tells a unique and well-communicated New England story.

Story Lines in the Darien Library Project

Three key story lines were prominent in the Darien planning: the library as a palace for the people, maintaining a place for "the quiet stir of thought," and creating the first of the twenty-first-century libraries. This mix of old and new, solid and flexible, provided a conceptual foundation for the building's themes, innovative space configuration and naming, and aggressive green building practices. A final, prominent part of the Darien Library planning was its emphasis on "the third place," a theme we also saw in the first three libraries reviewed in this chapter.

The Library as a Palace for the People

> [Architect] Peter Gisolfi talked about the Boston Public Library as sort of a palace for the people, [where] you go into the "popular" floor, and then you get drawn up into the sort of classic library.[30]

Based on this thinking, the planners had a three-level building in mind. First, the main level, with a "Main Street" story line that offered a busy, interactive community space for the popular library, the children's section, and a café. This busy space was not intended to be quiet and would create a themed experience based on the New England mill market concept.

Alan Gray, assistant director for operations at the library, referenced buildings such as Philadelphia's historic Head House and old New England mill buildings, where the outdoor marketplace extended inside through large, open spaces and an extension of the outside road into the inside flooring. The inside of the marketplace often had a brick floor to allow for the movement of heavy carts and lots of foot traffic. The Darien Library's entry area is designed to be reflective of these old-time community gathering spaces in a New England mill town.

> In a couple of areas, we were breaking new ground as far as we knew, with our concept of a "Main Street"—an active central area with all our new books, DVDs, and audiobooks on CD arranged as though in a store, with sidewalk displays, café tables, connecting the Children's Room on one side and the Community Room (a 170-seat auditorium), café, and fiction stacks on the other.[31]

Gray refers to the new book area as "the Shop" in an attempt to evoke the sense of being in an airport or on a busy street and passing by a bookshop.

> And then we actually have café tables along it—so that you can go get your coffee, sit right there, read a newspaper, meet your friends and talk. We have the self-checks there—so it is an active, busy place. People are passing by, and you have no expectation of quiet, and it's really quite

liberating. You can just do what you want to; kids can run back and forth . . . you can drop a wet umbrella, and so on.[32]

A final, more modern touch is the addition of flat-panel monitors to the space to display upcoming library events and programs.

The Quiet Stir of Thought

Just as the St. Paul Public Central Library planners were keenly aware of their patrons' love of the Central Library's classically designed physical space, the Darien planners were aware of the importance to their users of traditional library social spaces. They wanted to retain the friendly, warm feeling of their old library, allow for growth in an already extremely active customer service–driven library, and also provide opportunities for quiet reading and reflection. This traditional and timeless library function came to be called "the quiet stir of thought," a story line that originated with the twentieth-century library educator Jesse Shera's work.

Louise Parker Berry heard Shera speak early in her library career, and Shera's description of the importance of *the quiet stir of thought* has remained an important memory for her. "It stuck with her, and she wanted us to think about a part of the library where the quiet stir of thought could take place. We loved the sense of that—a place where an individual person could go" for reading, study, and reflection.[33]

Library for the Twenty-First Century

The lower level of the building was designed for the spaces where there would be the heaviest technology use by patrons. The public-access computing space is named the Power Library—a metaphor that includes not only the obvious meaning of electric power, but also a nod to information power through electronic access to resources.

> We knew what we wanted to achieve on the lower level, where we placed most of the building's patron technology: a Power Library. The Power Library is as close to a learning commons as we could make it—a central space with PCs, a tech training center, a SO/HO (small office/home office) copy and binding center, two smart conference rooms that can be upgraded to allow for videoconferencing, and the Teen Lounge, which is a hangout space with books, chairs, and some fairly robust computers that can drive a flat-panel wall display.[34]

The subtle use of language is a powerful tool in telling a very specific story throughout the library. For example, in addition to Main Street and the Power Library, adult reference is staffed with roving librarians and "touch-down spaces," where librarians and users work together using the librarians' laptops. They decided on a Welcome Desk rather than a circulation desk (circulation is conducted through self-checkout and automated returns), "pods" for reference points, and "glades" as a way of expressing the plan to reorganize the nonfiction collection into browsing areas somewhat divorced from Dewey.[35] This masterful use of language conveys a totally new way of working and truly responds to the need to keep current with the twenty-first-century consumer psyche.

Buildings as Community Stories

The four library building projects in this chapter are excellent case studies illustrating the potential of architecture and design to tell a story. Each of the libraries is physically and culturally reflective of its own unique community and was designed with those unique elements very much in mind. The buildings tell stories through their exteriors and their interiors, through design, theming, and language. Whether you are in line for an extensive building project or a simple redesign of an individual public space, consider the power of story to enhance your users' experiences.

Beware, however, of the temptation to select a story at random; the story must be authentic to *your* community. If people look at any library building project from a distance "and think they can map that local story onto *their* library and get the same effect, it becomes very superficial, because it's not embedded in the community."[36]

Darien wanted to keep a timeless feel to its new library building, not losing the strong sense of tradition; it built a new, traditional library with technology embedded throughout. St. Paul, on the other hand, took a prized historical building and made it feel more contemporary through the redesign of its interior spaces and through embedded technologies. Loyola University Chicago built a space reflective of twenty-first-century academic information behaviors and its own unique location on Lake Michigan's waterfront. The Cerritos Public Library has a Disney story line that is appropriate for its own community but would wear thin outside of Southern California, where there is a strong community match to that story line.

Ultimately, it's not about finding a story that you like and creating spaces reflective of that idea. It's about finding the story of your own community and creating spaces that fit your own community, its history, and its vision for itself.

Notes

1. Daniel Libeskind, www.daniel-libeskind.com/.
2. Daniel Libeskind, "17 Words of Architectural Inspiration," TED Talk, 2009, www.ted.com/talks/daniel_libeskind_s_17_words_of_architectural_inspiration.html.
3. Ibid.
4. Nancy Pickering Thomas, "Reading Libraries: An Interpretive Study of Discursive Practices in Library Architecture and the Interactional Construction of Personal Identity" (dissertation, Rutgers University, New Brunswick, NJ, 1996).
5. Jeffrey Scherer, interviewed by Kate Marek, September 22, 2009.
6. Ray Oldenburg, *The Great Good Place* (New York: Marlowe, 1989, 1997). This material is taken from pages xvii–xix and 20–42.
7. Jeffrey Scherer, interviewed by Kate Marek, September 22, 2009.
8. The projects' lead architects were Peter Gisolfi of Peter Gisolfi Associates (Darien Library), James Nardini of Charles Walton Associates (Cerritos Public Library), Devon Patterson of Solomon, Cordwell, Buenz (Loyola University Chicago Information Commons), and Jeffrey Scherer of Meyer, Scherer and Rockcastle (St. Paul Public Central Library renovation).
9. Cerritos Public Library, "Library History," http://menu.ci.cerritos.ca.us/collections/local_history/cl_libraryHistory.htm.
10. Waynn Pearson, "Epilogue," in *Last One Out Turn Off the Lights: Is This the Future of American and Canadian Libraries?* by Susan E. Cleyle and Louise M. McGillis (Lanham, MD: Scarecrow, 2005), 217.
11. John Hench and Peggy Van Pelt, *Designing Disney: Imagineering and the Art of the Show* (New York: Disney Editions, 2003), 1.
12. Bob Thomas, *Walt Disney: An American Original* (New York: Simon and Schuster, 1976).
13. Waynn Pearson, interviewed by Kate Marek, July 30, 2009.
14. Don Buckley, interviewed by Kate Marek, July 23, 2009.
15. Waynn Pearson, interviewed by Kate Marek, July 30, 2009.
16. Debbie Willms, interviewed by Kate Marek, August 14, 2009.
17. Ibid.
18. St. Paul Public Central Library, "Central Library History," www.stpaul.lib.mn.us/locations/central-history.html.
19. Jeffrey Scherer, interviewed by Kate Marek, September 22, 2009.
20. Ibid.

21. Sam Demas and Jeffrey A. Scherer, "Esprit de Place: Maintaining and Designing Library Buildings to Provide Transcendent Spaces," *American Libraries* 33, no. 4 (April 2002): 65–68.

22. Robert Seal, interviewed by Kate Marek, July 31, 2009.

23. Ibid.

24. Loyola University Chicago, "The Information Commons at Loyola University Chicago," http://libraries.luc.edu/about/ic/ic-overview.htm.

25. Robert Seal, interviewed by Kate Marek, July 31, 2009.

26. Ibid.

27. Loyola University Chicago, "Information Commons at Loyola University Chicago."

28. Rebecca Miller, "New Library Opens in Darien, CT; First LEED Gold Library Building in Region," *Library Journal,* www.libraryjournal.com/lj/community /buildingandfacilities/853876-266/new_library_opens_in_darien.html.csp.

29. Alan Gray, interviewed by Kate Marek, August 5, 2009.

30. Ibid.

31. Louise Parker Berry and Alan Kirk Gray, "State of the Art in Darien," *Library Journal,* Spring 2009 Library by Design: 1–9; also available online at www.libraryjournal.com /article/CA6656755.html.

32. Alan Gray, interviewed by Kate Marek, August 5, 2009.

33. Ibid.

34. Parker Berry and Gray, "State of the Art in Darien," 2.

35. Ibid., 9.

36. Jeffrey Scherer, interviewed by Kate Marek, September 22, 2009.

chapter six
DEVELOPING THE SKILL SET

Beware the well-told story.
—Stephen Denning

I HOPE BY now you've felt a real spark of interest in organizational storytelling. Maybe you're attracted by the idea of creating a sacred bundle of stories for your library, or perhaps you'd like to try to share a little more of your own personal library story with your staff and colleagues. Maybe you're on the brink of a building expansion or renovation, and you'd like to tell the story of your community through your building design. Whatever your interest in organizational storytelling, I hope this final chapter will give you some concrete tools to begin or expand your skills.

To get started, here are some general processes and principles I have learned through my reading about and practice with organizational storytelling. Later in the chapter I will review some specific story types along with their most effective uses. Finally, I will include a section on story triggers and general storytelling skills.

General Process and Principles

- Be thoughtful.
- Listen to those around you.

- Be authentic.
- Consider your audience.
- Consider your goals.
- What do you want to communicate?
- Take notes.
- "Index" for mental storage and retrieval.
- Use story triggers.
- Write drafts.
- Learning the story; remember the most important things.
- Practice!
    ... By yourself
    ... With a partner
    ... With small-stakes audiences

Be Thoughtful and Listen to Those around You

With the rapid pace of today's life, it is hard to take time just to reflect on the day and your experiences. Librarians are typically stereotyped as being introverted and introspective, but even those tendencies are not the same as intentional reflection. Being thoughtful is the mindset; listening to those around you is the action step.

Listening is a common theme in storytelling manuals. Although this may at first seem counterintuitive, it makes perfect sense. Before you can connect to people through stories, you must understand *their* stories—where they come from and how they got to their own points of reference. Time and again you can see that you must listen to what is around you so that you can connect to others; listening is also how you grow as a human being. So when you are new to an organization, for example, you truly listen to the sacred bundle stories to help you learn the legacy and values of that new place.

Listening is also a skill that can be developed and extended into greater depth. *Listening with the third ear* describes an action where we are not just listening to what people say, but being truly aware of the whole person as he speaks.[1] This includes noticing—and remembering—body language, overall demeanor, and other indications of the subtext of a person's comments. The benefits of listening with the third ear hold true for personal relationships as well, including dating, friendships, marriage, and parenting. Listening with the third ear means you can remember what a person has told you, and when you next talk you can build on past conversations. A simple "How's your aunt?" when you pass someone in the hall reconnects you to a colleague who told you last week about her aunt's accident; if you are paying attention and can use this moment to connect to another person, you can truly build a relationship. Ultimately people are much more likely to listen to you if you first truly listen to them.

I included Jack Maguire's "three Rs" of good listening in chapter 1, and they are worth repeating here.

- Remain silent until the other person has finished speaking.
- Respond with appropriate verbal and nonverbal cues.
- Remind yourself afterward of what you've heard that day.[2]

As Annette Simmons says, genuine listening may feel risky, "but you don't abdicate decision-making just because you slow down and completely process another person's point of view."[3]

Be Authentic

This common theme does not go away. It's important to consistently remember that your actions must match your stories. It is not helpful to ask about Aunt Mary's health if you are known to be fairly stoic yourself and not likely to sympathize with her sprained ankle. Connect with people based on true shared interests and backgrounds, whether that be home repair, sailing, or common parental frustrations with the local PTA. Authenticity means that when you "listen with the third ear" you are also actually caring about the person's response and truly believe in the relationships you are building. People can spot insincerity, and they can tell when you don't respect them enough to be genuine.

In terms of storytelling, however, being "authentic" does not necessarily imply that you can only use *true* stories. Even stories from your own past don't have to be spot-on accurate. The authentic nature of a story comes from its consistency with you as the teller, with the organizational values that you talk about, and with the reality of the vision about which you speak.

Consider Your Audience

The first two parts of the process, being thoughtful and listening, help you better understand your audience. Who are they, and what are their concerns? Just as we are beginning to understand the need to build library services based on user needs rather than our own perceptions of their needs, you should tell stories with a keen sense of what your listeners are ready to hear. For example, telling a story about the value of strong customer service would be a mismatch for a library staff that are full of confusion and hostility over last month's closing of a much-loved neighborhood branch.

Consider Your Goals

For natural storytellers, this is not a significant issue, as those persons are apt to use stories as a frequent part of their regular conversations. But for someone just beginning to incorporate stories into conversations and presentations, this is an important step. Effective storytelling doesn't just mean incorporating a humorous vignette at the beginning of a speech. You may also want to be careful not to overdo the story thing at the beginning. You may want to build community, spark action, or share values; each of these goals will require a different kind of story. For example, a springboard story is great for sparking action, but a "who I am" story is better for a new leader who wants to build trust.

What do you want to communicate? Listen to yourself: What stories are you telling all the time? Is it: I'm stressed, sad, annoyed, or is it: I'm optimistic, happy, joyful about the future, and so on? Be aware of the persistent messages you send through your daily chatting and the stories you choose to tell. You may be selecting those stories unconsciously, but they are there. Are those messages truly the ones you want to be sending, or could you be more intentional about your messages?

Take Notes

Don't underestimate the value of a written record of your observations. Jack Maguire includes recording your impressions as a central part of listening, and journaling is known to be a useful tool for memory and reflection.

Whether you do this at various points in the day, every day in the evening, or on a more sporadic schedule, remembering events and impressions and then capturing them in writing is extremely beneficial. If you don't feel comfortable with the concept of journaling, think of this process in more pragmatic terms such as a "work log" or "daily notes." However it makes sense to you, capture your thoughts and impressions in writing.

"Index" for Mental Storage and Retrieval

In the same vein, find a meaningful way to mentally store and retrieve events that you can build into stories or existing stories you'd like to use in the workplace. Terrence Gargiulo is especially explicit about the importance of creating a mental index for your stories so that you can use them more effectively. Indeed, indexing is among his "nine competencies" for organizational storytelling, which also include eliciting, listening, observing, synthesizing, reflecting, selecting, telling, and modeling.[4]

Gargiulo recommends a chronological life index as one way to categorize your stories, and general theming as a second way. Examples of themes are major events, influences, decisions, changes, successes, failures, disappointments, and significant people.

Once you've looked at your personal history in this way and formed some categories of stories, you can use story triggers to begin to fill in the details of those experiences and truly build stories to share effectively.

Use Story Triggers

Often the problem of "what stories to tell" gets in the way of a person wanting to build skills in organizational storytelling. But developing an index of stories helps to identify some significant events in your life that have been most meaningful. The general idea of story triggers is to take those starting points, using them to help generate story ideas through further reflection. These emotional and environmental prompts can really help you jump-start your storytelling. I will talk a little more about story triggers later in this chapter.

Write Drafts

It's very helpful at this point to begin to put your ideas on paper. Once you have an outline of some key events you'd like to develop into stories, begin to build a story in your mind, and then move it to paper. The writing process helps you to identify which parts of the story you find important and how the story elements fit together.

Learning the Story

There are various approaches to learning a story, just as there are individual learning styles. One method is to visualize a series of images, similar to what you might think of as a visual storyboard for a movie. Another way is to sketch a general outline of the story and focus on the key points. Certainly memorization is an option, but dependence on a memorized story can disconnect you from your audience by inhibiting your spontaneity and interactions.

Storytelling instructor Doug Lipman discourages memorization, particularly as a first step. Focusing too much on the words of the story rather than its interconnected events and meanings can be counterproductive. It's not the words themselves that are the essential nature of the story, but what Lipman calls the "most important things" (MITs).[5] Examples of the MITs for Lipman are what he loves most about the story, what draws him to the story, what the story is about for him, what the story means to him, and what he most wants to communicate through the story.

Here's a very short folk tale that serves as an excellent exercise for debating a story's MIT for an individual or a group.

The Wise Woman's Stone

A wise woman who was traveling in the mountains found a precious stone in a stream. The next day she met another traveler who was hungry, and the wise woman opened her bag to share her food. The hungry traveler saw the precious stone in the wise woman's bag, admired it, and asked the wise woman to give it to him. The wise woman did so without hesitation.

The traveler left, rejoicing in his good fortune. He knew the jewel was worth enough to give him security for the rest of his life.

But a few days later he came back, searching for the wise woman. When he found her, he returned the stone and said, "I have been thinking. I know how valuable this stone is, but I give it back to you in the hope that you can give me something much more precious. If you can, give me what you have within you that enabled you to give me the stone." (Author unknown)

Is the most important thing the generosity of the woman? The true knowledge of what's important in life? Is the MIT of this story trying to decide what the woman herself sees as the essence of life? Or is the MIT the immaturity and quest of the young traveler?

Reflecting on the MIT, Lipman says, helps a storyteller remember the story as revealed in its events, characters, and relationships, as well as the story's overall structure. You can add storyboarded mental images of the tale to further enhance your memory.

Practice

Lipman encourages repeated informal tellings of a new story as the first step in learning it. He reminds us that the idea of "practicing" a story frequently makes us think we should be doing something alone. That's a good first step, but it carries some of the same problems that flat memorization of the text brings: too much focus on an "inflexible version" of the story. Practice a little bit by yourself, a little bit with a partner, and a little bit with small-stakes, informal audiences.

Ask for feedback but not necessarily a "critique"—you are not in the business of entertainment, but in the business of sharing experiences and communicating meaning. "Beware the well-told story," Denning warns us. Too much polish and too many details may turn your story into a performance rather than a workplace communication.

Specific Story Types for Organizational Storytelling

Most of us have a basic understanding of general story types and genres. Story types include, for example, parables, folk tales, and myths and legends. Broad categories of organizational narratives were discussed in chapter 1, such as Boje's beginning, middle, and end tales. In this section, I look more specifically at the work of Stephen Denning and Annette Simmons with regard to the types of stories they recommend for effective use in daily work for communication and for leadership. Some of these story types have been described in earlier chapters, including Denning's springboard story and Simmons's "who I am" story, so this chapter will serve as a review of those examples. Note that these two authors stress many of the same concepts as they help us learn more about the effective use of storytelling at work. And keep in mind that while both Denning and Simmons tend to concentrate on stories for leadership, don't forget the implicit emphasis on "influence." You can develop your skills to influence people no matter what your position in the organization.

Denning's Storytelling Catalog

Stephen Denning emphasizes that the purpose of telling a story will determine the story's form. The traditional story form as outlined by Aristotle includes complex characters, a plot, and a reversal of fortune with a lesson learned. Denning calls this model with its associated rich detail the "maximalist" account. In organizational storytelling, however, there are many other ways to tell a story. Remember the photocopier repair technicians from *The Social Life of Information,* whose casual conversations about their work helped us to recognize the business value of shared experiences? These are examples of "boring" stories without traditional plots that can be quite effective for a certain purpose and a certain audience. These kinds of stories are similar to the business case study model, where examples are used that match the challenges of a specific audience, and the story listener can clearly see himself in the action. Here is a brief synopsis of Denning's storytelling catalog, which includes stories used for the following purposes:[6]

- sparking action
- communicating who you are
- transmitting values
- fostering collaboration
- taming the grapevine
- sharing knowledge
- leading people into the future

Sparking Action

Denning's classic "springboard story" fits into this category. Such a story should enable people to see the need for change as well as the possibility that it could indeed be successfully implemented. Denning recommends that you start with an actual event and limit the amount of detail in the telling so that the listener can create her own "mental space" to imagine a successful local outcome.

Communicating Who You Are

Trust is essential for good leadership. You must build trust in order to lead people through tough times such as constant white water or economic crisis. Denning suggests that to build trust, people need to know who you are, where you've come from, and how you developed your values and views. Effective stories in this category should be true vignettes from your past that show some strength, vulnerability, or specific lessons learned. These stories can include more development than Denning's springboard stories, as the detail and context of your own life will add richness to the impact of the story.

Transmitting Values

Stories in this category would be similar to the sacred bundle stories discussed in chapter 2, where leaders can communicate aspects of organizational culture based on "where we've come from, where we are, and where we're headed." Denning also suggests stories in parable form for communicating values, in which the characters and events do not necessarily directly parallel your own history.

Fostering Collaboration

Developing a shared narrative is another powerful organizational tool that can start simply through encouraging conversation. "One approach is to generate a common narrative around a group's concerns and goals, beginning with a story told by one member of the group. Ideally, that first story sparks another, which sparks another."[7] As the process continues, members of the group develop a shared perspective through this sharing of stories. To start this cycle of sharing, Denning suggests an open agenda that starts with one person sharing a story that touches on other persons' similar concerns or successes.

Taming the Grapevine

Stories flow through the workplace in good and bad ways, and rumors can be difficult to deal with. Denning encourages "harnessing the energy of the grapevine" to counteract destructive rumors and working with, instead of against, the underground flow of information. An effective way to do this is to interject something humorous into the rumor that highlights an untruth or incongruity in it. Then let the grapevine do its work.

Sharing Knowledge

Getting people to share knowledge may be difficult, and much of an organization's tacit knowledge can be lost without a way to capture what its employees know about their jobs. Moving from informal conversations about problem resolution and daily work to a systematic mechanism for knowledge capture is perpetually challenging. Denning suggests that a leader solicit knowledge-sharing stories through formal and informal structures, similar to the photocopier technicians' coffee breaks.

Leading People into the Future

It's hard to create a story about the future when the future is unknown. Denning suggests stories in this category that evoke a desired future, but that don't include specific details that could easily turn out to be wrong. The stories should allow for individual imagination and interpretation, similar to the springboard stories discussed earlier.

Simmons's Six Stories You Need to Know How to Tell

Annette Simmons's story categories are similar to Denning's in many ways, although there are unique aspects as well. Her books on organizational storytelling emphasize the potential of stories to influence people in positive ways, toward action and toward shared mission.

Simmons's six kinds of stories that everyone needs and that deserve your attention are presented in her book *The Story Factor*.[8]

- "who I am" stories
- "why I am here" stories
- "the vision" stories

- "teaching" stories
- "values-in-action" stories
- "I know what you are thinking" stories

The examples in this book from librarians Sylvia Jenkins and Carolyn Anthony beautifully illustrate Simmons's list of stories that everyone needs to know how to tell. As you read her list, remember those examples and think of how you could use your own personal stories more effectively in each category.

"Who I Am" Stories

Just as Denning emphasizes in his "communicating who you are" stories, Simmons stresses the importance of building trust among your listeners. Before people will truly listen to you as a leader, they will want to know who you are and what your own motivations are. A story helps you share parts of your background, your experiences, and your influences. This could include stories from your childhood, college, work experience, marriage, parenthood, military experience, and you as a library consumer or customer. The "who I am" story will begin to merge into the "why I am here" story.

"Why I Am Here" Stories

People want to know your motivations as a leader. Are you in it for the money? Are you planning to take over the library and fire all the middle management people in the first six weeks? The "why I am here" story is one area where Simmons and others emphasize that a story about you will be told, whether or not you are the one telling it. As a leader, you may have both personal and professional reasons for taking a new job—you want to advance professionally, but you also want to serve in a challenging community with rapid demographic changes. Think of a story that illustrates your passion for equity of access to information, for example. The "why I am here" story then leads directly into "the vision" story.

"The Vision" Stories

Once the listeners get to know you and trust you, they are likely to be open to hearing your ideas for the future. Remember that in an organization, this future will include them, so the listeners' buy-in is essential for success. Your vision should be one that can be shared by everyone to make a better future, similar in many ways to the vision Spartacus communicated to his army. This is especially true in service organizations such as libraries, where there is a great deal of potential to tap the natural inclinations of workers to create a better future for our customers.

"Teaching" Stories

Stories in this category can cover many different areas, from teaching specific skills such as a new automated circulation system to teaching new employees about organizational culture. Simmons describes stories as perfect tools for combining the *what* and the *how* of teaching—showing people what you want them to learn and how you want it done in the larger context. People may understand what you want them to do, but not why you want them to do it, building in resentment and frustration. Teaching, Simmons says, is a special kind of influence. "A Teaching story transports your listener into an experience that lets him or her feel, touch, hear, see, taste, and smell excellent performance."[9] The story has the potential to show how new behaviors can produce new results.

Teaching stories also lead to Simmons's next category of story: "values-in-action" stories.

"Values-in-Action" Stories

Workers today don't want to be told what to do, but rather to be inspired toward action through some common goals and aspirations. Telling stories is a great way to provide an example of a desired behavior or goal without being pedantic or instructional. We saw that beautifully illustrated in the examples in chapter 2, where library leaders did such an excellent job of communicating shared values of customer service, lifelong learning, and intellectual freedom.

"I Know What You Are Thinking" Stories

Simmons says it's not hard to predict how people might respond to your message as a leader. When trying to influence people, "unspoken objections" are easy to discover through simple research and your existing knowledge of your audience. By jumping on these emerging objections early in the game, Simmons says you can diffuse objections. By naming the objections first, you can often control a situation in danger of moving off track. In libraries we are not alone in combating the "that won't work here" point of view. Simmons encourages us to use our knowledge of that attitude when it exists and to employ stories to bring the attitude out into the open, so it can be discussed and dispelled.

These examples from Stephen Denning and Annette Simmons provide us with some basic starting points from which to begin to think more broadly about the potential of story to communicate in the workplace. There are many other ways to create examples and to categorize various uses of narrative in organizations. Scenario building, for example, is an excellent tool for planning that involves creating stories of alternate organizational futures. Another broad category of stories is "stories that heal," as described beautifully by Lewis Mehl-Madrona in his book *Coyote Wisdom*.[10] I have seen stories used in software-authoring teams; constructing stories of users' expectations for the new software can help generate ideas and development.[11] And a wonderful use of a story in the workplace can be as simple as invoking a metaphor, such as "He's all hat and no cattle." Enough said!

Story Triggers

Finding ways to generate stories from within, so to speak, can be challenging. Simmons lists several ways to generate ideas for all the story types she describes.[12]

Four Buckets of Stories

- A time you shined—Tell a story about a time you really got it right.
- A time you blew it—Tell a story about a time you really got it wrong!
- A mentor—Everyone has a mentor. Talking about yours reveals a little more about what you value and helps others remember their own personal heroes.
- A book, movie, or current event—Select something from a current movie, for example, that you want to highlight as part of what you value. A great illustration is the 2009 movie *Julie and Julia;* you could reference Julia Child's passion for her work and joy of life as something to which we should all aspire.

There are many more books and websites available that describe methods for creating personal stories. For example, Jack Maguire's book *The Power of Personal Storytelling* is full of excellent ideas for effectively using your life experiences to create stories. Another resource I've enjoyed is Joe Lambert's *Digital Storytelling Cookbook*. Lambert suggests a lifelong "memory box" to help assist in the indexing and storage of memories. "Images, videos, sounds, and other representations of events from our life can help us to reconstruct more complete memories and therefore expand the repertoire of story that we can put to use."[13]

Photographs and Memories

The most effective "story triggers" come from your own life experiences, and using photographs to bring memories to life is frequently mentioned as an effective story trigger. It has proven very effective for me to dig out an old photo and begin to assemble memories around the image. For example, I've been thinking about trying to capture some of my father's stories while I still have the opportunity, and when I rediscovered an old black-and-white photo from the late 1950s I used it to elicit a few stories from him about those years. What is equally effective in a related way is to "dig out" an image from my mind, from my memory, and to begin to fill in the story.

People often hesitate to tell stories from their childhood or from the distant past because they don't remember things clearly enough, and they have a fear of being inaccurate. Jack Maguire, a strong advocate of personal storytelling, encourages us to "do the best that we can with our imagination, or the story will never be told."[14] Maguire references storyteller Donald Davis, who talks about storytelling as creating a painting rather than taking a photo. The essence of the memory will be present, but will include your own individual nuances, expressions, and interpretations.

To begin to practice this, think of a memory and begin to fill in the details of the outline. Jack Maguire said, "I used to think I didn't have many personal stories to tell because I didn't have many clear memories. Now I know it was the other way around: I didn't have many clear memories because I didn't tell many personal stories."[15]

"Just Tell Them What Happened"

The power of an individual story, when you just tell people what happened, was illustrated earlier in this book by Carolyn Anthony's story about the woman who attended the library's Great Book discussions all of her adult life. By just telling her story in a cohesive but not necessarily dramatic way, the library patron shared a powerful message with her listeners. Carolyn Anthony was then able to retell the story in other contexts, adding to the story's tremendous power to communicate the value of the library in an individual's life.

Ira Glass, Peabody Award–winning broadcaster and host of the radio program *This American Life,* calls this simple sequence-of-events narrative an "anecdote," a story in its simplest form. Through relating events, the story builds a natural momentum. The anecdote, combined with shaping the story through natural questions of "what happened next," and with the final component of a moment of reflection toward a bigger point, creates a story experience that is larger than the sum of its parts.[16]

Examples of this kind of conversational storytelling are easy to find these days on the radio and on the Web. Many radio programs focus on people sharing anecdotes about their lives through interviews, news features, and special radio events. Some of my own favorites, all available through National Public Radio, are *Fresh Air, StoryCorps, Krista Tippett on Being, Bob Edward's Weekend,* and the previously mentioned *This American Life.*

An excellent web-based resource is TED: Ideas Worth Spreading. TED is an amazing organization that brings big thinkers together to share their stories. The website is full of digital recordings of people sharing their stories with a live audience. One of my favorites is Jacqueline Novogratz's story of a blue sweater her uncle gave her when she was a child, which after years of loving wear she donated to Goodwill. As a young woman later in life, Novogratz was in Africa when she spotted her blue sweater being worn by a young boy in the hills of Rwanda.[17] Although this could remain a simple personal memory, Novogratz tells this powerful story widely to illustrate the tremendous interconnectedness between all of us throughout the world. Although not everyone has the experience of finding connections to their lives across the globe, everyone does have many experiences that, when shared, will resonate deeply with others.

Collecting Stories

Finally, don't forget to collect stories from others, including your service population. Soliciting stories from others can be as easy as leaving a comment form at the circulation desk or inviting users' stories via your blog. The American Library Association hosts creative essay contests about users' unique experiences at libraries, and this could be easily replicated at the local level.[18] Invite participation in building your local library story. Trust the value of those stories and practice using them effectively.

Stylistic Advice

Parallel to the advice to "just tell the story" is to *be yourself*. Each person has his or her own personal style in life; some people are musicians, some are readers, some are great cooks. As you gain confidence in sharing stories you will feel more confident in your own style, but there is no single way to tell stories to which you should aspire.

Simmons says to choose stories that communicate your message, that you enjoy telling, and that you would actually tell in real-life situations such as at a party or over dinner. She also says these must connect to *you* as the teller.

Denning and Simmons both stress brevity for stories in the work setting. Beware of TMI (too much information!), and beware of the "well-told story," which Denning says is too much obsession over traditional story detail and development. Instead, concentrate on keeping things personally relevant to your audience, leaving space in the story for individual buy-in through personal interpretation and finding common ground. If it feels right for you, use humor to brighten your story and emotion to add details about who you are.

And don't forget, the more you interact with people, the more stories you have to tell.

The Power and Potential of Organizational Storytelling

There is so much more to be said about stories and storytelling in organizations. There is a rich literature of folk tales and sacred bundle stories from every modern and historical culture throughout the world. There is research on the importance of literature to teaching and learning and on the value of stories for building bonds among people.

We have emerged from our industrialized culture into a new era of imagination and innovation. Stories are resurfacing as a valuable tool for all kinds of communication, including communication in the workplace. Through good times and bad times, stories can sustain us and can inspire us toward a vital future.

Stephen Denning's springboard story idea gives us a good model to think about telling stories in the workplace: "Storytelling in the workplace has been successful in many organizations, but we haven't yet maximized that potential here in this library. But . . . *what if we could?!*"

Notes

1. Theodor Reik takes the phrase "listening with the third ear" from Friedrich Nietzsche. Reik's explanation of the phrase and his own use of it are described in his book *Listening with the Third Ear* (New York: Farrar, Straus, and Giroux, 1948, 1983), 144.

2. Jack Maguire, *The Power of Personal Storytelling: Spinning Tales to Connect with Others* (New York: Jeremy P. Tarcher/Putnam, 1998), 231.

3. Annette Simmons, *Whoever Tells the Best Story Wins: How to Use Your Own Stories to Communicate with Power and Impact* (New York: American Management Association, 2007), 207.

4. Terrence L. Gargiulo, *The Strategic Use of Stories in Organizational Communication and Learning* (Armonk, NY: M. E. Sharpe, 2005), 3.

5. Doug Lipman, *Improving Your Storytelling: Beyond Basics for All Who Tell Stories in Work or Play* (Little Rock, AK: August House, 1999), 103–4.

6. Stephen Denning, "Telling Tales," *Harvard Business Review* 82, no. 5 (May 2004): 122–29.

7. Ibid., 126.

8. Annette Simmons, *The Story Factor: Inspiration, Influence, and Persuasion through the Art of Storytelling* (Cambridge, MA: Perseus, 2001), 1–26.

9. Simmons, *Whoever Tells the Best Story Wins*, 79.

10. Lewis Mehl-Madrona, *Coyote Wisdom: The Power of Story in Healing* (Rochester, VT: Bear, 2005).

11. Mike Cohn, *User Stories Applied for Agile Software Development* (Boston: Addison-Wesley, 2004).

12. Simmons, *Whoever Tells the Best Story Wins*, 39.

13. Joe Lambert, *The Digital Storytelling Cookbook* (Berkeley, CA: Center for Digital Storytelling, 2010), 7.

14. Maguire, *Power of Personal Storytelling*, 24.

15. Ibid., 16.

16. Ira Glass, "Ira Glass on Storytelling 1," www.youtube.com/watch?v=n7KQ4vkiNUk.

17. Jacqueline Novogratz, "Investing in Ending Poverty," TED Video, August 17, 2009, http://blog.ted.com/2009/08/investing_in_en.php.

18. "At My Library Creative Essay Contest," www.atyourlibrary.org/essay-contest.

resources

ORGANIZATIONAL STORYTELLING

Armstrong, David M. *Managing by Storying Around: A New Method of Leadership.* New York: Armstrong International, 1999.

Boje, David. *Storytelling Organizations.* Thousand Oaks, CA: Sage, 2008.

Brown, John Seely, Stephen Denning, Katalina Groh, and Laurence Prusak. *Storytelling in Organizations: Why Storytelling Is Transforming 21st Century Organizations and Management.* Burlington, MA: Elsevier Butterworth-Heinemann, 2005.

Clark, Evelyn. *Around the Corporate Campfire: How Great Leaders Use Stories to Inspire Action.* Sammamish, WA: C&C, 2004.

Cohn, Mike. *User Stories Applied for Agile Software Development.* Boston: Addison-Wesley, 2004.

Denning, Stephen. *The Leader's Guide to Storytelling.* San Francisco: Jossey-Bass, 2005.

_____. *The Secret Language of Leadership: How Leaders Inspire Action through Narrative.* San Francisco: John Wiley, 2007.

_____. *The Springboard: How Storytelling Ignites Action in Knowledge-Era Organizations.* Boston: Butterworth-Heinemann, 2001.

_____. *Squirrel, Inc.: A Fable of Leadership through Storytelling*. San Francisco: Jossey-Bass, 2004.

_____. "Telling Tales." *Harvard Business Review* 82, no. 5 (May 2004): 122–29.

Gabriel, Yiannis. *Storytelling in Organizations: Facts, Fictions, and Fantasies*. New York: Oxford University Press, 2000.

Gargiulo, Terrence L. *The Strategic Use of Stories in Organizational Communication and Learning*. Armonk, NY: M. E. Sharpe, 2005.

Hale, Martha. "Stories in the Workplace." *Public Libraries* 42, no. 3 (May/June 2002): 166–70.

Marek, Kate. "The Role of Organizational Storytelling in Successful Project Management." In *Convergence of Project Management and Knowledge Management,* ed. T. Kanti Srikantaiah, Michael Koenig, and Suliman Hawamdeh (Lanham, MD: Scarecrow, 2010).

Neuhauser, Peg. *Corporate Legends and Lore*. Austin, TX: PCN Associates, 1993.

Simmons, Annette. *The Story Factor: Inspiration, Influence, and Persuasion through the Art of Storytelling*. Cambridge, MA: Perseus, 2001.

_____. *Whoever Tells the Best Story Wins: How to Use Your Own Stories to Communicate with Power and Impact*. New York: American Management Association, 2007.

BUILDING STORYTELLING SKILLS

Glass, Ira. "Ira Glass on Storytelling 1." www.youtube.com/watch?v=n7KQ4vkiNUk.

Greene, Elin, and Janice del Negro. *Storytelling: Art and Technique*. Santa Barbara, CA: Libraries Unlimited, 2010.

Lambert, Joe. *The Digital Storytelling Cookbook*. Berkeley, CA: Center for Digital Storytelling, 2010.

Lipman, Doug. *Improving Your Storytelling: Beyond Basics for All Who Tell Stories in Work or Play*. Little Rock, AK: August House, 1999.

Maguire, Jack. *The Power of Personal Storytelling: Spinning Tales to Connect with Others*. New York: Jeremy P. Tarcher/Putnam, 1998.

Mehl-Madrona, Lewis. *Coyote Wisdom: The Power of Story in Healing*. Rochester, VT: Bear, 2005.

National Storytelling Network. www.storynet.org.

GENERAL RELATED RESOURCES

Block, Marylaine. *The Thriving Library: Successful Strategies for Challenging Times.* Medford, NJ: Information Today, 2007.

Block, Peter. *Community: The Structure of Belonging.* San Francisco: BK, 2008.

Boekesteijn, Erik. "Discover Innovations at DOK, Holland's 'Library Concept Center.'" *Marketing Library Services* 22, no. 2 (March/April 2008), available online at www.infotoday.com/MLS/mar08/Boekesteijn.shtml.

Bridges, William. *Managing Change: Making the Most of Transitions,* 2nd ed. Cambridge, MA: De Capo, 2003.

Brophy, Peter. "Telling the Story: Qualitative Approaches to Measuring the Performance of Emerging Library Services." *Performance Measurement and Metrics* 9, no. 1 (2008): 7–17.

Brown, John Seely, and Paul Duguid. *The Social Life of Information.* Boston: Harvard Business School Press, 2000.

Brown, Karen, and Kate Marek. "Librarianship and Change: A Consideration of Weick's 'Drop Your Tools' Metaphor." *Library Administration and Management* 19, no. 2 (Spring 2005): 68–74.

Cohen, Dan S. *The Heart of Change Field Guide.* Boston: Harvard Business School Press, 2005.

Demas, Sam, and Jeffrey A. Scherer. "Esprit de Place: Maintaining and Designing Library Buildings to Provide Transcendent Spaces." *American Libraries* 33, no. 4 (April 2002): 65–68.

Fulford, Robert. *The Triumph of Narrative: Storytelling in the Age of Mass Culture.* New York: Broadway Books, 2000.

Giesecke, Joan, ed. *Scenario Planning for Libraries.* Chicago: American Library Association, 1998.

Green, Melanie C., Jeffrey J. Strange, and Timothy C. Brock, eds. *Narrative Impact: Social and Cognitive Foundations.* Mahwah, NJ: Lawrence Erlbaum Associates, 2002.

Haven, Kendall. *Story Proof: The Science behind the Startling Power of Story.* Westport, CT: Libraries Unlimited, 2007.

Heath, Chip, and Dan Heath. *Made to Stick: Why Some Ideas Survive and Others Die.* New York: Random House, 2007.

Hench, John, and Peggy Van Pelt. *Designing Disney: Imagineering and the Art of the Show.* New York: Disney Editions. 2003.

Hess, Jeffrey A., and Paul Clifford Larson. *St. Paul's Architecture: A History.* Minneapolis: University of Minnesota Press, 2006.

Hochberg, Ilene. *Who Stole My Cheese?* Philadelphia: Running, 2003.

Kotter, John P. "Introduction." In *The Heart of Change Field Guide,* by Dan S. Cohen. Boston: Harvard Business School Press, 2005.

Kotter, John P., and Dan S. Cohen. *The Heart of Change.* Boston: Harvard Business School Press, 2002.

Kotter, John P., and Holger Rathgeber. *Our Iceberg Is Melting: Changing and Succeeding under Any Conditions.* New York: St. Martin's, 2005.

La Vida Biblioteca. "Living Library." http://lavidabiblioteca.blogspot.com/2008/10/living-library.html.

Libeskind, Daniel. "17 Words of Architectural Inspiration." TED Talk, 2009. www.ted.com/talks/daniel_libeskind_s_17_words_of_architectural_inspiration.html.

Living Library Projects. http://living-library.org/.

Meyer, Danny. *Setting the Table: The Transforming Power of Hospitality in Business.* New York: HarperCollins, 2006.

Miller, Rebecca. "New Library Opens in Darien, CT; First LEED Gold Library Building in Region." *Library Journal.* www.libraryjournal.com/lj/community/buildingandfacilities/853876-266/new_library_opens_in_darien.html.csp.

"New Market, Philadelphia, Pennsylvania." Wikipedia. http://en.wikipedia.org/wiki/New_Market_(Philadelphia,_Pennsylvania).

Novogratz, Jacqueline. *The Blue Sweater: Bridging the Gap between Rich and Poor in an Interconnected World.* New York: Rodale, 2009.

_____. "Investing in Ending Poverty." TED Video, August 17, 2009. http://blog.ted.com/2009/08/investing_in_en.php.

Oder, Norman. "'Living Library' Débuts in Santa Monica." *Library Journal* 133, no. 19 (November 15, 2008): 15.

Oldenburg, Ray. *The Great Good Place.* New York: Marlowe, 1989, 1997.

Parker Berry, Louise, and Alan Kirk Gray. "State of the Art in Darien." *Library Journal,* Spring 2009 Library by Design: 1–9. Also available online at www.libraryjournal.com/article/CA6656755.html.

Pearson, Waynn. "Epilogue." In *Last One Out Turn Off the Lights: Is This the Future of American and Canadian Libraries?* by Susan E. Cleyle and Louise M. McGillis, 215–20. Lanham, MD: Scarecrow, 2005.

Pine, B. Joseph, II, and James H. Gilmore. *The Experience Economy: Work Is Theatre and Every Business a Stage.* Boston: Harvard Business School Press, 1999.

Putnam, Robert. "Bowling Alone: America's Declining Social Capital." *Journal of Democracy* 6, no. 1 (1995): 65–78.

_____. *Bowling Alone: The Collapse and Revival of American Community.* New York: Simon and Schuster, 2000.

Reik, Theodor. *Listening with the Third Ear: The Inner Experience of a Psychoanalyst.* New York: Farrar, Straus, and Giroux, 1948, 1983.

Rice-Oxley, Mark. "Borrow a Muslim? A 'Living Library' to Prick Stereotypes." *Christian Science Monitor,* June 4, 2008.

Schon, Donald A. *Beyond the Stable State.* New York: W. W. Norton, 1971.

Senge, Peter. *The Fifth Discipline: The Art and Practice of the Learning Organization.* New York: Doubleday, 1990.

Shera, Jesse. "The Quiet Stir of Thought, or, What the Computer Cannot Do." *Library Journal* 94, no. 15 (September 1, 1969): 2875–80.

Thomas, Bob. *Walt Disney: An American Original.* New York: Simon and Schuster, 1976.

Thomas, Nancy Pickering. "Reading Libraries: An Interpretive Study of Discursive Practices in Library Architecture and the Interactional Construction of Personal Identity." Dissertation, Rutgers University, New Brunswick, NJ, 1996.

WebJunction. "Living Library Projects." Webinar, July 22, 2009. www.webjunction.org.

Weick, Karl E. "Drop Your Tools: An Allegory for Organizational Studies." *Administrative Science Quarterly* 41 (July 1996): 301–13.

_____. *Sensemaking in Organizations.* Thousand Oaks, CA: Sage, 1995.

Zander, Rosamund, and Benjamin Zander. *The Art of Possibility.* New York: Penguin, 2002.

index

You may also be interested in

BE A GREAT BOSS:
ONE YEAR TO SUCCESS
Catherine Hakala-Ausperk

To help library managers improve their skills and acumen, renowned speaker and trainer Catherine Hakala-Ausperk presents a handy self-study guide to the dynamic role of being a boss. This workbook is organized in 52 modules, designed to cover a year of weekly sessions but easily adaptable for any pace.

ISBN: 978-0-8389-1068-9 / 232 PGS / 8.5" × 11"

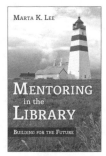

MENTORING IN THE LIBRARY:
BUILDING FOR THE FUTURE
Marta K. Lee

Noted reference librarian and researcher Marta K. Lee offers librarians at all levels both her experience and her ideas about establishing a formal mentoring process at the library.

ISBN: 978-0-8389-3593-4 / 136 PGS / 6" × 9"

COACHING IN THE LIBRARY:
A MANAGEMENT STRATEGY FOR
ACHIEVING EXCELLENCE,
SECOND EDITION
Ruth F. Metz

Experienced librarian and coach Ruth Metz outlines a focused and results-oriented plan for achieving the best results from staff members through a coaching style of management.

ISBN: 978-0-8389-1037-5 / 120 PGS / 8.5" × 11"

SUCCESSION PLANNING
IN THE LIBRARY:
DEVELOPING LEADERS,
MANAGING CHANGE
Paula M. Singer with Gail Griffith

Drawing on her expertise as a leading consultant on human resource issues in the library, Paula Singer addresses the often fraught issue of planning for change at all levels of an organization.

ISBN: 978-0-8389-1036-8 / 160 PGS / 8.5" × 11"

Order today at www.alastore.ala.org or 866-746-7252!

ALA Store purchases fund advocacy, awareness, and accreditation programs for library professionals worldwide.